JESUS BAPTISES I̱ SPIRIT

Jesus Baptises in One Holy Spirit

Who? How? When? Why?

David Pawson

ANCHOR RECORDINGS

**This edition published in Great Britain in 2014 by
Anchor Recordings Ltd
72, The Street, Kennington, Ashford TN24 9HS**

**For more of David Pawson's teaching,
including MP3s, DVDs and CDs, go to
www.davidpawson.com
For further information, email:
info@davidpawsonministry.com**

ISBN 978-1909886452

Printed by CreateSpace

Contents

Foreword

It is both a delight and an honour to write the Foreword for this important new book by David Pawson.

David and I have known each other for several years now. Every time we have met, there has been a very real sense of iron sharpening iron – of two people refining their theological views in the light of the friendly criticisms which each has offered. That being the case, I would like to state here and now that I have always found David's views on my writings and on my public teaching to be extremely sharp and helpful.

Nowhere has this been more true than in the aftermath to the publication of my book, *Explaining Baptism in the Holy Spirit*. David was kind enough to say how much he appreciated my work on the biblical texts relating to this topic, and at the same time he was passionate enough about the subject to share his misgivings about my application of them!

My own view was this: that the doctrine of 'baptism in the Holy Spirit' is essential for normative, biblical Christianity. More precisely, I took the position (which I will always hold) that every person who wants to become a true follower of Christ must repent of their sins, believe in the Lord Jesus Christ, and be baptised in both water and the Holy Spirit. I argued that full and effective initiation into the kingdom of God must necessarily involve all these aspects of regeneration.

I also argued that the experience of being baptised in the Holy Spirit is an intensive, immersive and invasive one. I showed that the word *baptise* comes from the Greek verb *baptizo* which literally means 'to saturate entirely'. Having said that, I then made the mistake of opting for what David Pawson calls the 'time-bomb' theory of Spirit baptism. In other words, I proposed two things: first, that it is possible, when we are converted, to be baptised in the Holy Spirit without realising it; second, that the full realisation of this experience can happen later as the Spirit, given at our conversion-initiation, is 'released' in power at a later date.

David immediately spotted the inconsistency here. He expressed his critique in the following way: 'If baptism in the Holy Spirit is "an intensive, immersive and invasive experience", how can it happen without the recipient knowing that it's happened? How can we really have been baptised in the Holy Spirit if that experience does not involve being "entirely saturated in God's empowering presence"?'

Now that is a very pertinent and penetrating question. If I was ever to rewrite my book, I would certainly take this criticism into account and adjust my arguments accordingly. Indeed, today I would argue strongly that the time-bomb theory needs to go, and that we must ensure that every believer is as thoroughly baptised in the Holy Spirit as, in the New Testament, they are in water – i.e. by total immersion!

Happily (for my sake), I do not need to write such a book. In many ways, *Jesus Baptises in One Holy Spirit* represents what I should have written, and indeed so much more! In this present volume, David corrects my position and argues that evangelical Christianity needs urgently to restore baptism in the Holy Spirit to a central position in both its theology and praxis.

David and I share the view that this is especially vital for charismatic evangelicalism. In recent years, many Charismatics have lost sight of the very essence of their self-identity, which is wholly tied up with the baptism in the Holy Spirit and the subsequent expression of the *charismata*, or gifts of the Spirit. These two things lie at the very heart of what it means to be a charismatic Christian. Yet, in the 1990s, there are growing signs that Charismatics are neglecting these two emphases, and are putting other things (such as exotic 'manifestations') in their place. This is a very dangerous, subtle and unseen transition, and David's book is a timely plea for Charismatics to remember the rock from which they were hewn and to return to those things which mark their true self-identity.

So I want to nail my colours firmly to the mast and say that I agree wholeheartedly with what David says on p.195: that sacramentalists need to distinguish clearly between baptism in water and baptism in the Holy Spirit; that evangelicals need to distinguish clearly between believing in Jesus and receiving the Spirit; and that pentecostals need to relinquish the view that there are two receptions of the Spirit. What we need today is a comprehensive view of conversion-initiation which comprises repentance of sin, faith in Christ, water baptism, and receiving the gift of the Holy Spirit in power (the 'plunging' of which David speaks).

All this, finally, is of supreme importance as we approach the end of the millennium. There are signs all around us of a growing awakening in the nation – of more and more people seeking after God. There are signs, in short, of what some like to call 'revival'. If this is right (and I believe it is), then many people will be coming to faith in Christ in the years which lie ahead of us. If these new believers are to be effectively initiated into Christ, then it is of paramount importance that we put a very high value on the doctrine and experience of 'Spirit baptism'. It is vital to ensure that they experience the 'normal Christian birth'.

Dr Mark Stibbe, 1997

Prologue

I didn't like Whit Sunday. Every year I had to prepare two sermons on the Holy Spirit. Each time I scraped the barrel of my limited knowledge, which allowed only two approaches to the subject.

I could make it *historical*. Pentecost was the 'birthday' of the Church, an event not to be repeated but to be remembered. Parallels could be drawn between the Church and a spacecraft. After a fiery and noisy lift-off, she now floats serenely and silently in orbit. One hymn we sang about the Holy Spirit described his activity as 'soft as the breath of even'.

Or it could be *doctrinal*. From a number of books of systematic theology on my shelves, I could compile a list of the Holy Spirit's attributes and activities, always pointing out that he was the shy person of the Trinity who kept in the background and did not want attention drawn to himself.

It could not be *existential*. I had neither a conscious relationship with the Holy Spirit nor any direct experience of his power, so I could not draw on these for illustrations. Not that anyone would miss these missing dimensions: most of my hearers were in the same boat.

So I breathed a sigh of relief when the calendar moved on and I could return to preaching a gospel centred on the Father and the Son. Until next year!

However, this situation always left me vaguely uneasy. I felt that I should know more about the Holy Spirit, but it was only later that I realised I needed to know him personally.

I was certainly curious about him. As part of my postgraduate studies at Cambridge, I had set myself the task of writing a mini-thesis entitled 'What happened on the original day of Pentecost?' After studying all the relevant books in the college library, I wrote a paper with the naïve conclusion that nobody now knows. The scholars I consulted were so divided in their interpretations that I presumed the original event was too long ago and too far away for anyone to be sure. Such a sceptical finding would be acceptable to my tutor, provided I had done my homework. But it left me none the wiser.

Dissatisfaction with all this steadily built up to a climax. I resolved to preach my way out of my ignorance, and boldly announced to the congregation that I would preach a lengthy series of sermons about the Holy Spirit, working my way through every biblical reference to his person and work. I carefully planned to reach Acts on Whit Sunday.

I hoped to finish with my curiosity satisfied and my guilt removed. Little did I dream what the real result would be. Three personal encounters were to coincide (or was it coincidence?) with this extended exposition.

The first took place at Herne Bay Court Christian

Holiday Centre in Kent, at a conference for evangelical pastors. When I arrived, a friend who had already seen the rooming list warned me in a horrified whisper that I was 'sharing with someone who speaks in tongues'. He would have used the same tone of voice if he had spotted a crocodile in the bath! That evening I went upstairs with some trepidation, anticipating a disturbed night. I need not have feared. My room-mate was gentle, friendly and quiet (didn't even snore). Indeed, he seemed so ordinary, yet I knew that some extraordinary things had happened in the church he pastored (Basingstoke Baptist). My appetite was whetted, and I later visited Michael Pusey to find out more.

I lived quite near Stoke Poges (Gray's 'Elegy in a Country Churchyard' was written there), where there was an Anglican retreat house. Hearing of a small house-party who met to share about the Holy Spirit, I dropped in for one or two sessions. I remember meeting Michael Harper and Harry Greenwood. This was the early 1960s, and I was hearing about a rediscovery of 'Pentecost' in the mainline denominations. Up to that time, my experience had been limited to meeting their pastors in ministers' fraternals, where they kept very quiet about their distinctive beliefs and practices, presumably for the sake of ecumenical acceptance. Now I was getting to know about these things through people on the other side of the fence. I listened to 'tongues' and their interpretation for the first time. This was more like it.

The third encounter was nearer home. On our board of deacons was a man I can only describe as awkward.

He appeared to be the self-appointed leader of the opposition (does God put one in every church to keep the pastor humble?). He had a brilliant brain and could present persuasive arguments against my suggested changes. After frustrating church business meetings my wife would say: 'Don't mind him; the rest are with you.'

However, once a year I had a respite. He had a weak chest and was subject to hay fever in the late spring which could lead to severe lung congestion, putting him in bed for days, if not weeks. One such attack occurred when I was moving from the Old to the New Testament in my 'Holy Spirit' sermons.

I went to see him on a Sunday afternoon, and all the way there my mind kept thinking of James chapter 5. When I got there, James (for that was his name, usually changed to Jimmy) immediately asked me what I thought about James chapter 5, and whether I would anoint him for healing, since he had an important business appointment in Switzerland on the following Thursday. I said I'd pray about it (a pious evasion!).

On Wednesday, his wife rang and asked when I was coming. Not able to think of an excuse, I agreed to bring other church leaders with me that evening. I purchased a large bottle of olive oil and went into the church building to pray for a successful anointing, actually kneeling in the pulpit.

It is not easy to pray for the healing of someone you'd rather see confined to bed for another week or two! My mixed motives led to an argument with the Lord. How did I ever get into such a fix? If it didn't work, he'd be an even greater thorn in my flesh. And I couldn't heal him, anyway. I didn't have this Holy Spirit power yet. It would all go horribly wrong. My prayer dried up.

Quite suddenly, I began to pray for him with all my heart and soul. The words simply poured out – only not in English. Part of my brain said it sounded like Chinese. I remember glancing at my watch and thinking it must have stopped some time ago. I couldn't have been talking for a whole hour. I wondered if I could do it again – and found a very different language coming out of the same mouth.

The excitement was intellectual rather than emotional. So this is what happened in Acts 2. I was being baptised in the Holy Spirit. That meant power. Things were going to happen in Jimmy's bedroom that evening. I was sure of it.

In the event, we went about it in a very amateur way, working through the last part of James' epistle as if it was a car-servicing manual. It said we had to confess our sins to one another, so I told Jimmy I'd never liked him and he said it was mutual. Then I poured the oil all over his head, under the impression that the more we used the greater its effect. Then we all prayed, kneeling round his prone form. Guess what happened – absolutely nothing!

I couldn't think of anything to do or say next, so I beat a hasty retreat to the bedroom door. Just before disappearing, I stammered out: 'What time is your plane from Heathrow tomorrow morning? I'll run you to the airport.' Then I fled. I didn't sleep much that night, dreading to face his disappointment.

Nor did I contact him next day. He telephoned me – to tell me he was ready to be picked up. In the middle of the night it was as if two giant hands had squeezed his lungs and expelled all the fluid. He'd been to the doctor, who pronounced him fit to travel. He'd also been to get his hair cut, but the barber refused to start until he'd had a thorough shampoo ('the worst case of greasy hair I've seen').

Jimmy was free of that malady from then on. He and his wife were soon filled with the Spirit themselves. Above all, he became my closest friend and confidant in that fellowship. There had been more healing than I had dared to hope for. When later critics told me such happenings were the work of the devil, you can imagine my reaction.

But I did want to be sure that it was of God. The main test I used for most things was the revealed will of God in scripture. I was already studying this very theme for my sermons. Now it was all making sense, coming alive. The Father's promise, the Son's prayer and the Spirit's power were just the same as they'd always been in these 'last days' between Jesus' first and second comings to planet Earth.

On the following Sunday I got up to preach the next in the series, which had now reached the later chapters of John (all about the promised Comforter or Standby). I didn't feel any different, and most of my material had been prepared over the preceding weeks. But after the service a young man asked me: 'What's happened to you this week?' When I queried his reason for asking, I got a devastating but delightful reply: 'Last Sunday, you didn't know what you were talking about; this Sunday you do.' Ken is now a pastor himself.

The rest, as they say, is history. This new dimension to my ministry opened up new avenues of service but closed others. Having gained a reputation as an 'evangelical', I began to be suspected of becoming a 'charismatic'. One friend, a famous Bible teacher, asked me if I'd lost my critical faculties. The implication was that I'd substituted feelings for thought, experience for theology, Spirit for scripture.

This was both baffling and frustrating. The new experience had come together with a new understanding. Theology and experience were illuminating each other. I was studying scripture more than ever before, determined to discover what the Word said about the Spirit and finding, almost as a bonus, what the Spirit says about the Word. I could now identify with so many statements in the Bible, many of which I had hardly noticed before, considering them as references to a bygone era.

I have both explained and exercised 'spiritual gifts' since then (prophecy, healing, words of knowledge and wisdom), but the focus of my thinking has been that initial work of the Holy Spirit, often called 'baptism in the Spirit'. This is what I understood happened to me that day as I knelt alone. But that was seventeen years after 'accepting Christ' as my Lord and Saviour. Why did I have to wait so long? Do others have to? Do we have to grow spiritually to a certain stage before being eligible?

I remember asking an evangelist, David Shepherd, about this. In his broad Welsh accent, which cannot be reproduced on paper, he bellowed: 'Have you not noticed? The disciples were baptised in the Holy Spirit in Acts 2, not in Acts 28 – at the beginning, not at the end!' I'm not sure about his exegesis but the reply sent me back to my Bible with a different slant on things.

This book concentrates on the single subject of Spirit baptism, asking four questions in particular: WHO baptises and is baptised? HOW does it happen? WHEN should this take place? And, above all, WHY?

Inevitably, there is a limited overlap with two other books I have written, namely *The Normal Christian Birth* (recently reissued) and *Fourth Wave* (now out of print). Both looked at Spirit baptism in wider contexts. This study goes deeper and explores fresh territory by looking at the historical development of this doctrine.

The urge to put pen to paper again was stimulated by an astonishing reversal in very recent times. After a century of prominence, first outside the mainline denominations and then inside them, 'baptism in the Holy Spirit' is again falling out of the picture (this trend and the reasons for it are explored in Chapter 4).

Before this surprising decline is accepted, urgent questions need to be faced. Are we in danger of losing something vital? How fundamental is it to Christian living?

Undoubtedly, one confusing fact is the wide variety of opinion about it to be found within the Christian Church. There are some deep differences. Can they be reconciled?

With each other? With scripture?

I have a passion to see Word and Spirit brought together in harmony. I believe that theology must be translated into experience and that experience must be grounded in theology. Either without the other is a distortion of the Christian faith and vulnerable to serious error.

Some readers may be tempted to skip over or rush through the detailed exegesis of relevant scriptures (in chapters 2 and 3), driven by curiosity to see if they agree or disagree with my conclusions. But the roots of study are as important as the fruits, and both should be weighed and judged. In particular, I hope that those who struggle with the practical problems (faced in Chapter 7) will not let these difficulties have the last word in shaping their convictions, but will come back with me to the Bible so that God himself may have the final say.

Note: 'The Holy Spirit' is now a name for the third person of the Trinity, but I have varied this phrase to draw attention to the unfolding revelation in Scripture. 'Baptised in holy Spirit' is a literal translation of the Greek, without a definite article, indicating power rather than a person; and 'holy' with a small 'h' is used as an adjective to describe nature. The divine Spirit is always spelt with a capital 'S', whereas a small 's' refers to the human spirit. Later, I tend to use terms familiar in contemporary debates, like 'baptism in the Spirit' or even 'Spirit-baptism'. In every case, context has determined usage.

1

The Surprising Silence

Jesus was and is a baptist or, as it should be translated, a baptiser. He shared this title with his cousin. In fact, it was John who actually gave it to him, after John himself had been given it by the public.

JESUS' FORERUNNER

Nearer a nickname than a name, 'baptiser' was a kind of job description. The basic meaning of 'baptise' is to immerse a solid in a liquid. Since John was doing this to people in the Jordan river, it is hardly surprising that he became known as 'John the dipper' or 'John the plunger' – which is what our Bibles should say (unfortunately, most English versions don't translate the Greek into an equivalent word, only transliterate it into our letters).

John was doing it for a very simple reason – to get people cleaned up. Yet the Jordan, besides being the lowest river on earth, is also one of the muddiest, especially in its lower reaches just before it enters the Dead Sea. Naaman the leper was not the only one to find the dirty little stream an objectionable ablution!

But the object of the exercise was not physical cleanliness. John saw his baptism as a 'sacrament' (though he would not have used the word), a physical action with moral and spiritual results. In this case, past sins would be washed away, forgiven. The baptised would emerge from the river with a clean conscience.

This would not happen because of any special quality in the water, but because the God who told John to baptise would work a miracle when he did it. Not that this would happen automatically. It would only work for those who recognised their sins, were willing to name them in public confession and had acted in such a way as to prove they had truly repented of them, from renunciation to restitution. The miracle was not magical, but thoroughly moral.

The reason for John's activity was as simple as its object. The kingdom of God was at hand, The time was very near when God's rule would intervene in human affairs, as the people of God had longed to see for a very long time. But now it was coming, they were far from ready. A holy God would not overlook sin, particularly in his own nation. He would come with fire, burning up all that was ungodly.

John also knew that God would re-establish his kingdom on earth through a king like David – indeed, a son of David. John knew he himself was not that 'Messiah', nor did he discover that it was his own cousin until quite a late stage. But he saw himself as the one to prepare the way for him, the forerunner, the 'Elijah' before the 'Elisha'.

So John was calling the children of Israel back to the very place where they had crossed into the promised land of Canaan – to begin all over again, to make a clean start.

He was content with this ministry, happy to be a voice in the very wilderness where he had spent many solitary years in preparation. He had no ambitions for himself, ready as the best man to hand over the bride to the bridegroom, to become less as he would become greater.

He was, however, only too aware of the limitations of his ministry. For one thing, he performed no miracles of healing or exorcism. Even his mediating forgiveness of sins through baptism was not enough to meet the real need of sinning people.

He could free them from sins in their past but not protect them from sins in their future. He could get them clean but not keep them clean. He could minister remission of sins but not the removal of sin. In other words, the relief from guilt could only be temporary. They needed much more help than he could give them if there was to be a permanent cure for their stubborn self-centredness.

John simply didn't have the power to effect such a transformation in the lives of his hearers. But he knew someone who did. The very person for whom he was a forerunner was 'more powerful' and therefore worthy of greater honour. John did not feel qualified to untie his sandals (the job of the second-lowest slave; the very lowest of them had to wash the feet!).

There were two things this 'coming one' would do for sinners which no one else could do.

Lamb of God After John realised that his cousin Jesus was the one expected, he pointed him out with the memorable words: 'Look, the Lamb of God, who takes away the sin of the world!' (John 1:29). It is worth considering this statement in detail. It is an amazing claim.

Since John's followers were Jews, we may ask what associations this might arouse in their minds. They were familiar with the sacrifice of lambs to atone for sins, though these were mature animals with horns ('ram' would be a much better English equivalent). Others might think of the scapegoat carrying the sins of the people away into the wilderness. But both rams and goats had to be offered repeatedly, whereas John's statement has a finality about it – 'taken away' for good.

The surprising note is its universal application. John's ministry was to his own people, and their hopes for the future were often nationalistic. But here is an announcement without ethnic limits. The whole human race could be beneficiaries. The *goyim* (Gentiles) are all included.

Christians reading the claim tend to refer its fulfilment to Jesus' once-for-all sacrifice on the cross. But that application could be too limited. The verb 'takes away' is in the present continuous tense: 'who goes on taking away', which seems to point to an ongoing task that would extend through time and space, as indeed it has done and is doing. It will not stop until it has reached the ends of the earth and the end of the age.

Wonderful though this is, the thrust is essentially negative. What will be put in its place? What will fill the empty space in the human heart? What will prevent seven unclean spirits from re-inhabiting the clean but vacant property? John had a clear and compelling answer to such questions. His negative prediction was matched by a very positive promise.

Baptiser in Spirit The words for which John would be best remembered are quite straightforward: 'I baptise you in water, but he will baptise you in holy Spirit' (Mark 1:8).

We shall look at these words more carefully later (in Chapter 3) but we can make some preliminary observations here by asking again what John's Jewish hearers would make of them.

'Spirit' would not be new. Their history contained many examples of the Spirit of God, his invisible power, coming on ordinary men and women, enabling them to do extraordinary things (see Chapter 2 for a summary of the Spirit's activity in the Old Testament).

To be 'baptised' in Spirit would be a new idea. But the concept of being 'plunged' was now familiar through John's actions in the River Jordan. In some way the two baptisms would be analogous – an 'overwhelming' experience of being completely submerged in a fresh medium.

But the main emphasis in John's statement is on the

adjective 'holy'. English translations mistakenly insert the definite article ('the'), turning a description into a name. (I go into this more fully in Appendix 2 of *The Normal Christian Birth*.) John was promising they would be 'plunged in *holy* Spirit' – the real antidote to their sinful condition. The same person who took their sin away would soak them in holiness.

'Holy' was perfectly familiar to Jews. Their God was 'the Holy One of Israel' and their calling was to be holy as he was holy. To be a holy people meant to be a separated people – negatively, from sin; positively, for God. Not just clean, but clean enough for God's exclusive use.

This plunging in holy Spirit was by far the most prominent feature in John's preaching. Surprisingly, he only talked about the Lamb of God taking away the sin of the world on one occasion to a limited audience, but of 'baptism in Spirit' it is recorded: 'This was his message' (Mark 1:7 – lit. 'he kept preaching'). Regularly and repeatedly, he warned his disciples that a baptism in water for forgiveness of sins was not enough, but was all he could do for them. They must move on to another baptiser and another baptism or they would regress to their former condition. The clean beginning he had helped them to make would be wasted.

From this brief summary of the ministry of the forerunner who prepared the way for Jesus, we turn to an even briefer summary of how the followers of Jesus down through the succeeding centuries have echoed John's proclamation.

JESUS' FOLLOWERS

The reason for entitling this first chapter 'The Surprising Silence' will now become apparent. John's repeated emphasis on Jesus as baptiser in holy Spirit has been largely ignored during most periods of church history.

Ancient Looking back through the centuries, it is clear that the rest of John's ministry has been faithfully continued by the Christian Church. His practice of water baptism has been almost universal (the Quakers and the Salvation Army are among the few exceptions). It has to be added that there have been considerable changes in the who, how and why of it, but it is still being done.

His call for repentance, reformation and restitution is still heard. His offer of forgiveness for sins committed is still made, even considered the heart of the good news, the 'gospel'. His warning about judgment to come for those who continue in their sins has echoed, more or less, down through the years.

His identification of Jesus as 'the Lamb of God who takes away the sin of the world' has been widely incorporated into ecclesiastical liturgy, especially in the Eucharist, or Communion. It is repeated around the world every Sunday. But where is the ringing affirmation that Jesus is the baptiser in holy Spirit? It has been largely forgotten, overshadowed by his other titles and functions. He has been preached by most as Saviour and Lord, by many as Master and Friend, but by very few as Baptiser.

This has led to an imbalance, if not a distortion, of the gospel, of which I give two examples.

First, preaching has focused on the offer of forgiveness rather than the offer of holiness. In practice, ministry has gone little further than John's. He was able to get sinners baptised and forgiven. Is that all the Church can and should be doing? Of course, Christian pastors can point to the atonement of the cross as the ground of forgiveness and baptise in the name of Jesus (or the Trinity) – but, in practice, are the recipients of this any better off than John's disciples unless Jesus baptises them in holy Spirit? To put it another way, is holiness as necessary as forgiveness if we are one day to 'see the Lord' (Heb. 12:14)? Is forgiveness alone an adequate qualification for admission to heaven? (For an extended examination of this vital issue, see my book: *Once Saved, Always Saved? A study in perseverance and inheritance*, Hodder and Stoughton, 1996).

Second, preaching has focused on the past rather than the present work of Jesus, what he *did* for us rather that what he *does* for us. It is a pity that his ascension is remembered on a Thursday, not a Sunday, and is so often overlooked. That event is as important to Christian faith as his death, burial and resurrection, as every creed testifies. It was the inauguration of his present ministry as our High Priest at the right hand of God the Father. As well as interceding for us, preparing a place for us and exercising all authority in heaven and on earth, perhaps the most important role he now plays is to receive the promised Spirit from his Father and to pour out that same

Spirit on his disciples – not once, but time after time after time. Only he can baptise in holy Spirit, but he will continue to do so as long as this is needed.

It is a tragedy that this has not found a place in the creeds of the Church, as compared with forgiveness of sins. What Christ takes away has been proclaimed and accepted. What he gives in its place has been muted. That could be one reason why liturgies concentrate on 'miserable sinners' rather than joyful saints!

Of course, I do not mean to imply that the Church has been without the Holy Spirit altogether. He has been active, even when he has not been acknowledged. Those who have sought more than they were offered have received more. Many have been baptised in holy Spirit without fully understanding the connection between their experience and the biblical promise it was fulfilling. There have been 'Spirit-filled' saints in all ages, some recognised as such by the whole Church, most known only to their intimates and God.

Yet God alone knows how much more power, purity and unity would have characterised his people on earth had John's clear and confident message been faithfully proclaimed, with his emphasis on the positive as well as the negative.

If only the Church had been as sure as he was that the same Jesus who can take away our sin can also plunge us into holy Spirit, her history might have been very different.

But even God himself cannot change the past once it has happened, only the present and the future. The same applies to us. While we may express regret that this vital truth has been so long neglected, we have both the opportunity and the duty to repent of it and restore this vital dimension to our preaching and practice.

This long-standing neglect has provided one of the two motives for writing this book, but there is a much more recent development which has been decisive.

Modern Some readers may feel that this deficiency has already been remedied or is at least well on the way to being met. Surely the twentieth century witnessed a rediscovery of 'baptism in the Spirit' on a scale unknown in any previous century? The growth of pentecostalism into the 'third force in Christendom' (alongside Catholics and evangelicals) is sufficient evidence of this.

All this is true. We shall later trace (in Chapter 5) the gradual disappearance of 'baptism in the Spirit' during the first few centuries of church history and its gradual reappearance during the last few centuries, from the Puritans to the pentecostals. And the twentieth century saw the greatest change, beginning on its very first day: January 1st 1901. Baptism in the Spirit, accompanied by speaking in tongues, as in the days of the apostles, was sought and found on that day and has since spread to millions around the world.

For the first fifty years, this rediscovery was repudiated by and excluded from the existing church bodies, causing it to find expression in new denominations, regarded by many as sects or even cults. Orthodox evangelical in doctrine, they preached a 'foursquare' gospel about Jesus as Saviour, Lord, Baptiser and King.

In the second half of the twentieth century, 'baptism in the Spirit' and its promoters gained access to the other denominations and quickly spread through their ranks. It looked as if this recovered dimension would again become normal throughout the Church.

But it didn't. The last decade or so has seen a reversal, in both the old and the new churches. Clear witness to Spirit-baptism has shrunk back to the pentecostals, and has even begun to fade among some of them.

The major reason for this rejection is theological. The experience was at first welcomed back into the Church, but the doctrine associated with it was not. Many felt that it was a far from adequate interpretation of all the relevant biblical data. They could not square pentecostal teaching with scripture.

The fact is that at no stage in this recovery were all the dimensions of the New Testament understanding of baptism in the Spirit fully integrated (as we shall see in Chapters 4 and 5). This failure made the whole issue vulnerable to criticism, which for various reasons was destructive rather than constructive.

However, the issue will not go away. The pentecostal wing is growing very rapidly and is likely to be the dominant pattern of the Church in the twenty-first century, particularly in the developing nations.

There is, therefore, a double need for a thorough re-examination of Spirit-baptism. Both those who have become silent and those who are still speaking need to be called back to a fully integrated appreciation of the biblical concept, if deep division is to be avoided.

As long ago as 1993, I wrote a 'Study Paper Pull-out' for the magazine *Renewal* (Issue No. 206) entitled: 'Whatever happened to baptism in the Spirit?' This book is an expanded version of that article.

The first step is to look into the Bible itself, beginning with the Old Testament. John's announcement was not made in a vacuum. He was the last in a line of prophets who had experienced for themselves and explained to others the workings of the Spirit of God.

2

The Prophetic Promise

It may seem strange that a book on 'baptism in the Holy Spirit' should include a whole chapter on the Old Testament, since the phrase is nowhere to be found in it. But John, the first person to use it, was speaking to Jews, not Gentiles. They were a people with a history and John's preaching was building on what they already knew, as all good instruction must. Their past was enshrined in their scriptures and in these may be found the seeds of what became explicit in the New Testament.

'Baptised' was certainly a new word, coined for John's practice of immersion, but Jews were already familiar with ritual washing and bathing. The 'sacramental' use of water to achieve inner and spiritual cleansing would not be a surprise, but drawing an analogy between water and Spirit as the medium probably would be.

'Spirit' would be the most well-known word, usually referred to as 'the Spirit of God' or, since they used his name in this connection, 'the Spirit of Yahweh'. Most of our study will concentrate on this.

'Holy', as an adjective qualifying 'Spirit', is comparatively rare in Hebrew. Indeed, there are only three references (Ps. 51:11; Isa. 63:10, 11; all concerned with sin and rebellion and the grief they cause). But many, many times God is described as holy. He is 'the Holy One of Israel', particularly in Isaiah's prophecies. And the law of Moses repeatedly reminds his people that their calling is to 'be holy as he is holy' (e.g. Lev. 19:2). The notion that the Spirit of God shares this attribute with him would be unusual but not incongruous. However, the major emphasis in their thinking would be the *power* rather than the *purity* of God's Spirit.

The root of their understanding lay in their conviction, based on their past, that God is *living*. This means far more than his existence. He is active in this world, both in word and deed. A dead God would not cease to be but would no longer be saying and doing things in time and space (this is precisely what the modern 'God is dead' philosophy believes). Dead people are the same: they go on existing in the world of disembodied spirits ('Sheol' in Hebrew; 'Hades' in Greek), but are no longer around or active in this world.

The mark of life is breath. Dead persons have stopped breathing. The invisible movement of air through nostrils and mouth is the sign and source of animation. It is significantly the carrier of all speech, all verbal communication between persons.

The Spirit of God is the breath of God, enabling him to speak and act in this world.

In both Hebrew and Greek the word for breath, wind and spirit is the same, invisible but moving. Whereas Greek has only one word (*pneuma*), Hebrew uses two. One is for normal, quiet breathing, of which we are not conscious (*neshemah*), the other is for strong, heavy breathing, of which we are only too aware (*ruach*, an onomatopoeic word which sounds the same as its meaning, like 'splash'; 'ch' is pronounced as in the Scottish 'loch' – the word cannot be spoken without audible breath). When applied to the wind, the two words indicate the difference between a gentle breeze and a howling gale.

It is the stronger word that is used for God's Spirit, invisible but audible and immensely powerful. We could sum it up as three 'M's: might, movement, and mouth. It expresses the thoughts that God is almighty, that he is on the move and that he communicates with his creatures. 'Spirit of God' is interchangeable with 'hand of God', particularly in the prophecies of Ezekiel. What we can do with our hands, he can do through his Spirit or breath. It was the 'blast of his nostrils' which divided the Red Sea as a 'strong east wind'. When he blows, the grass withers and the flowers fall, his breath being hot. He can breathe fire, flames of judgment. Even hyperventilation is ascribed to him, 'snorting with anger'. Perhaps Ezekiel's vision of the valley of dry bones is the most typical illustration of all this. God tells him to prophesy to the 'wind' and bones become bodies, then to do it again and 'breath' enters them. It is very obvious that the real power is the Spirit of God. The vision is reminiscent of the creation of Adam.

In fact, the creation of our planet was the work of the Spirit. Genesis 1 contains the first ten commandments issuing from God's heavenly throne. But they were not given until there was someone on earth to hear and obey them. The Spirit was hovering (brooding?) just above the liquid chaos and it was through him that the earth was first made habitable and then inhabited. The Spirit was and is the executive member of the Godhead, applying the words of heaven to the events of earth. When Isaiah asked: 'Who has directed the Spirit of the Lord?' (40:13), he was thinking more about the divine muscle than his mind, the power rather than the plan.

All this is supremely true of human beings, the climax of creation. 'Let *us* [surely addressed to Son and Spirit] make man in our own image' (Gen. 1:26). The animals are described as 'living souls' (the Hebrew equivalent of 'breathing beings'); now man joins them, a special creature into whose clay body God breathes life (Gen. 2:7; the word here is the quiet, normal breath). Job is right to cry: 'The Spirit of God has made me; the breath of the Almighty gives me life' (33:4).

The Spirit of God is not only the power in creation but also over creation, whether inanimate or animate, whether dividing the Red Sea or giving Balaam's ass the power of speech. But most of his recorded actions are to do with human beings. There is a wide variety of expressions for this empowering. He can 'come upon' them, 'rest upon' them, be 'given to' them, 'appear on' them – and many others.

As he enables God's will to be done on earth, he also enables human beings to do it. He can take over their minds and bodies, working in, with and through them to accomplish the divine purposes.

But, and it is a very important 'but', the Spirit works by co-operation, not imposition. The power is voluntarily received and used, never forced on anyone. This comes out very clearly in the sad and sordid history of society after the 'fall' of Adam and Eve in the garden of Eden, followed by the perverted sexual intercourse between male angels and female humans (Gen. 6:1-2; 'sons of God' are interpreted as angels in the book of Enoch, referred to in 2 Peter and Jude), which was as offensive to God as relations between humans and animals (Exod. 22:19). This unholy alliance introduced unclean spirits and occultism and led to a decadent and degraded outlook. 'The Lord saw how great man's wickedness on the earth had become, and that *every* inclination of the thoughts of his heart was *only* evil *all* the time' (Gen. 6:5).

God's reaction to this total corruption is highly significant: 'My Spirit will not *contend* with man for ever' (Gen. 6:3). This clearly indicates that God would not use his sovereign power to override the free choice which he had given. He would respect their wills (or their won'ts!) by not imposing his will on them, other than by limiting the length of their lives, thus preventing the perpetuation of their pollution of his creation.

He will 'strive' or 'contend' with them – seeking to persuade them, by deed as well as word, to live according to his will. But he will never force them. There will be a time limit to this striving, as well as to their opportunity of responding. His patience can run out. His anger can boil over. And when his Spirit gives up, fearful consequences follow. Restraint is removed, wickedness knows no bounds and society self-destructs. Universal violence is just one result (Gen. 6:11).

From this brief summary of the Spirit's dealings with creation and creatures and with the human race as a whole, we turn to his particular relation with the people God chose to be both the demonstration and the mediation of his desire to save people from such a dreadful fate.

THE KINGDOM OF ISRAEL

From beginning to end of their national history, examples of God's Spirit acting through human beings are contrasted with others operating within the limits of their own strengths. The comparison is often described in terms of human 'flesh' and divine 'Spirit'. What the flesh cannot achieve, the Spirit can. Zechariah summed it up: '"Not by [military] might nor by [political] power, but by my Spirit," says the Lord Almighty' (Zech. 4:6).

In other words, what human beings cannot reach with all their natural abilities and resources can be reached when they can tap supernatural power. Ordinary people can attain extraordinary heights. Conversely, it is impossible to fulfil God's will without the aid of God's Spirit.

We may analyse the Old Testament data under three headings. When the Spirit of God 'clothed himself' with a person, he or she could do, be or say what otherwise they could never have done, been or said.

To do the impossible Here we look at the *physical* realm, feats beyond natural strength or skill.

The first example is the building of the tabernacle in the wilderness. God gave a very detailed specification, but no plans or drawings! As well as the mental grasp of his concept, numerous physical skills would be required – wood-carving, metal-casting, gold-plating and cloth-embroidering among them. Anything less than perfect would be discarded as unworthy of God's dwelling-place. As slaves in Egypt, the Israelites had done little except make bricks (with and without straw), but no bricks were needed now. The Spirit of God came on two men, Bezalel and Oholiab, giving them both the skills and the oversight of a construction team. Their heads mastered and their hands applied exactly what was in the mind of God (Exod. 31:1-11; 35:30-5). Centuries later, King David conceived the plan of the Temple in the same way (1 Chron. 28:12).

Samson is an example of strength rather than skill – brute force, we would say today – not always wisely used. Sunday school pictures are highly misleading when they portray him as Macho Man with bulging biceps. Had he looked like that, Delilah would never have asked him what the 'secret' was! He was only able to kill lions and carry away city gates when the Spirit came on him. When the Spirit departed from him, after his Nazarite vow not to cut his hair was broken, he was as weak as anyone else when outnumbered. It was the returning Spirit rather than the regrown hair that enabled him to deal a greater blow to Israel's enemies in his death than in his life.

The Spirit was the source of miracles, as well as might. Physical events going well beyond the normal course of nature accompanied the heroes of Israel's heritage. The interviews between Moses and Pharaoh and the plagues that followed them spring to mind. But the clearest examples are found in the lives of Elijah and Elisha. Elijah stopped the rain for years, and called down fire from heaven that could melt stones (I have held in my hand a piece of the altar he built on Carmel, a piece of ordinary limestone fused into dark green crystal by intense heat).

When Elisha expressed his ambition to have a 'double portion' of the Spirit Elijah had, he was not asking for twice the power. In those days, when a father's estate was divided among his sons, the eldest got twice as much as the others because he inherited the responsibility of looking after the family and the business. Elisha was asking to be Elijah's 'son and heir'. However, he performed some sensational miracles, including feeding thousands with a few loaves of bread and raising the dead.

One of the most extraordinary powers of the Spirit was to transfer a person from one place to another without any means of transport, something twice mentioned in connection with Elijah (1 Kgs 18:12; 2 Kgs 2:16) and many times for Ezekiel (e.g. 3:10-15; from Jerusalem to Tel Aviv, but the one in Babylon!). Philip provides a New Testament parallel (Acts 8:39-40).

In passing, we may mention another skill given by the Spirit – music, given uniquely to King David, but also to many others, in both vocal and instrumental form.

However, this is moving beyond the merely physical and we will look at this again later, in another connection.

This section can finish where it began, with building. After the return from exile in Babylon, the ruined temple in Jerusalem was reconstructed, though on a smaller scale and in fits and starts. Haggai and Zechariah encouraged and rebuked the workers. Zerubbabel, surviving prince of the royal line of David, laid the foundation stone. As proof that God was with them and would enable the work to be completed, Zechariah predicted that Zerubbabel would single-handedly lift the final capstone into place! He added: 'Then you will know that the Lord Almighty has sent me to you' (Zech. 4:9). This amazing feat is the primary reference in the text quoted earlier: 'Not by might nor by power, but by my Spirit', though few preachers give it a physical application.

So let's move on to some other demonstrations of supernatural abilities available in the Spirit.

To be the unattainable We are moving from the physical into the *social* realm. A society is usually as good, or as bad, as its leaders. This is clearly the case with Israel.

Leadership is a highly skilled calling. There is a delicate balance to be achieved between dictatorship on the one hand and democracy on the other, between a leader imposing his own will through tyranny and surrendering to the wills of his followers. Leaders can easily be too strong or too weak. Wisdom is the ability to avoid both extremes.

Leadership in Israel went through different phases, in each of which the Spirit gave the necessary qualifications.

As Isaiah put it: 'He will be a spirit of justice to those who sit in judgment' (Isa. 28:6).

The patriarchs (Abraham, Isaac and Jacob) came first and are described by God as 'my anointed ones' (1 Chron. 16:22). Throughout the Bible, oil is a symbol of the Spirit and 'anointed' a description of one on whom the Spirit rests. In Hebrew the word is *mashiach*, hence our word 'Messiah' (compare 'Christ', from the Greek word for anointing, *chrisma*).

Moses brought the Israelites out of Egypt by the power of the Spirit on him, and the same Spirit was later given to the seventy elders who shared the responsibility with him (Num. 11:17). Joshua brought them into the land of Canaan, having received the Spirit when Moses laid hands on him (Num. 27:15-21), an anointing that gave him authority and, more significantly, wisdom to use it rightly (Deut. 34:9).

Later, whenever the people sinned, were invaded by foreigners as punishment, repented and cried to the Lord for help, he raised up 'judges' to deliver them, all given abnormal abilities of different kinds by the Spirit. This is specifically mentioned with Othniel (Judg. 3:10), Gideon (Judg. 6:34), Jephthah (Judg. 11:29) and Samson (Judg. 13:25).

When the people demanded a king like other nations, Samuel reluctantly anointed the first, Saul, who was the people's choice. The Spirit 'rushed mightily upon him' (1 Sam. 11:6) but, alas, like Samson, departed from him later leaving an empty heart for evil spirits to enter. The second, David, was God's choice and when he was anointed, the Spirit was transferred from Saul to him (1 Sam. 16:13). The third and last king of the united kingdom was Solomon, who asked for and received the gift of wisdom. The answer to his prayer came in the famous incident when he settled a dispute between two prostitutes claiming the same baby.

The civil war after his death divided the people into two kingdoms. Significantly, no 'anointing' is mentioned from then on, nor is the Spirit. There were more bad kings than good, particularly among the ten tribes of 'Israel' in the north. After steady decline in moral and spiritual character, they were taken off to Assyria. The two tribes of 'Judah' in the south were exiled to Babylon not long afterwards. The Spirit had long since departed and left them to their own resources, which meant that they were no match for the superpowers on their borders.

But the nation was resurrected, as Ezekiel's vision of dry bones had indicated. They returned and rebuilt, under the leadership of Joshua the priest and Zerubbabel the prince. Zechariah the prophet had a vision of two olive trees feeding oil into a gold lampstand, and was told: 'These are the two who are anointed to serve the Lord of all the earth' (Zech. 4:14).

Sadly, the next centuries saw the decline and eventual disappearance of Spirit-anointed leadership, and the nation lost its independence to Persian, Syrian, Egyptian, Greek and finally Roman overlords.

There is, however, a third strand of the Spirit's work in human beings, which was perhaps the most significant in the history of Israel.

To say the inconceivable From the physical and social, we turn to the *verbal* gifts. By far the major part of the Spirit's activity in the Old Testament is in the form of supernatural speech, enabling men and women to say what God wanted to say. The phrase 'Thus says the LORD [i.e. Yahweh]' occurs nearly four thousand times. A person used by the Spirit in this way was called a 'prophet' or 'prophetess'.

The first to be given this title are the patriarchs, Abraham, Isaac and Jacob (1 Chron. 16:22). Their two-way conversations with God are a striking feature in their stories, highlighting the obvious fact that prophecy involves the ability to hear from God before being able to speak for God.

Moses was supremely a prophet, a model for '*the* prophet' who would come later (Deut. 18:15; John 1:21; 6:14; 7:40). When the seventy elders were appointed to share his responsibilities, the Spirit on him was shared with them and 'they prophesied, but they did not do so again' (Num. 11:25; though the last part could be translated: 'and continued to do so'). At the same time, two other men at the other side of the camp, Eldad and Medad, also prophesied. The newly appointed elders, jealous for their new position, objected and demanded discipline, but the large-hearted Moses responded with: 'I wish that all the Lord's people were prophets and that the Lord would put his Spirit on them' (Num. 11:29) – an aspiration that would not be fulfilled until 'baptism in the Spirit' became available in the New Testament Church.

The extraordinary story of Balaam demonstrates the

power of the Spirit to put prophetic words into the mouth of a Gentile fortune-teller (Num. 23:7-10; 24:2-9) and even into the mouth of his donkey (Num. 22:28-30)! Caiaphas presents an interesting parallel in the New Testament (John 11:49-52).

Among the charismatic judges, Deborah was a prophetess, as Miriam, the sister of Moses, had been before her and Huldah would be after her.

The prophet Samuel marked the transition of Israel to a monarchy, and both the first kings of Israel were prophets. When the Spirit came on Saul, 'turning him into another man', he had just met a 'procession of prophets . . . and he joined in their prophesying' (1 Sam. 10:10-11). We are not told exactly what this consisted of, but we can say with certainty that coming from his mouth were words which God was giving him. Whether this was accompanied by bodily movements (leaping or dancing?) we cannot say, though it is interesting to note that others '*saw* him prophesying' and coined the saying: 'Is Saul also among the prophets?' On a later occasion he certainly gave visible as well as audible evidence of the Spirit's possession – by stripping off his clothes and prophesying in Samuel's presence, giving a further boost to the popular saying (1 Sam. 19:23-4).

The same kind of behaviour overtook three groups of Saul's agents, despatched to arrest the outlawed David, as soon as they encountered Samuel and his prophets (1 Sam. 19:18-21). It seems that prophesying was infectious!

David played many roles in his life – shepherd, soldier

and sovereign among them. But when he reached the end of his life, the uppermost function in his mind was: 'The Spirit of the LORD [Yahweh] spoke through me; his word was on my tongue' (2 Sam. 23:2; compare Peter's statement on the day of Pentecost that 'the patriarch David . . . was a prophet' Acts 2:29-30).

In the same 'last words' of this, the greatest king Israel ever had, David describes himself as 'the man *anointed* by the God of Jacob, Israel's singer of songs' (2 Sam. 23:1; the last phrase could also be 'beloved singer' or 'sweet singer', as in the Authorized Version). This is a suitable point to comment on the close connection between prophecy and music.

Many, many prophecies in the Old Testament are in poetry rather than prose (it is useful to have a Bible that differentiates by print layout). Of course, it is Hebrew poetry, 'parallelism', which depends on couplets saying the same thing twice in different ways, with some rhythm (4.3 is the most common 'beat') but little rhyme. Reading the Psalms aloud and antiphonally (two people or groups taking alternate 'lines') helps to recover the poetic qualities.

More important, poetry is the language of the heart, whereas prose goes to the head. Poetry conveys feelings rather than thoughts and in the case of poetic prophecy communicates the feelings of God (try reading Hosea 2 without a catch in your voice).

And poetry is more easily set to music than prose, making the message even more memorable. God himself is musical; he rejoices over his people with singing (Zeph.

3:17). Not surprisingly, most of David's prophecies are in the form of songs, particularly those concerning his 'Messianic' successor, whom he looked up to as his 'lord (Ps. 110:1, the most frequently quoted OT verse in the NT).

David was also careful to see that the prophetic gifting was at the heart of the nation's worship. He always appointed 'seers' (who received prophecy in the form of pictures or visions) as his choirmasters. Asaph, Herman and Jeduthun, and 288 of their relatives, were 'trained and skilled in music' for 'the ministry of *prophesying* accompanied by harps, lyres and cymbals' (1 Chron. 25:1).

Music can stimulate as well as communicate prophecy. Elisha would ask a minstrel to play until the Spirit came on him (2 Kgs. 3:15). This complex relationship between music and the Spirit continues into the New Testament ('Be filled with the Spirit. Speak to one another with psalms, hymns and spiritual songs. Sing and make music in your heart to the Lord' Eph. 5:18-19).

To return to the prophets as such, most specifically attribute their gift to the Spirit. Micah sums up their function in Israel: 'As for me, I am filled with power, with the Spirit of the LORD, and with justice and might, to declare to Jacob his transgression, to Israel his sin' (Mic. 3:8). Such a message required courage: their boldness was also the work of the Spirit.

Some prophets on whom the Spirit came are not very well known, like Azariah (2 Chron. 15:1) and Micaiah (2 Chron. 18:23). Others were simply priests who prophesied, like Jahaziel, a Levite (2 Chron. 20:14) and Zechariah, son of a priest (2 Chron. 24:20).

The three best-known, with the longest ministries, were Isaiah ('Now the sovereign LORD has sent me with his Spirit' Isa. 48:16), Jeremiah and Ezekiel (who kept falling to the ground in the presence of the Lord, but the Spirit lifted him to his feet again – Ezekiel 3:24 – note that he didn't need supernatural power to push him down but to raise him up!).

Let the post-exilic prophet, Zechariah, sum it up. He reminded his hearers of the pre-exilic 'words which the LORD [Yahweh] of hosts had sent by his Spirit through the former prophets' (Zech. 7:12). From the same period, Nehemiah's public prayer of confession on behalf of his stubborn nation contains significant insights into the prophetic role: 'For many years you were patient with them. By your Spirit you admonished them through your prophets. Yet they paid no attention, so you handed them over to the neighbouring peoples' (Neh. 9:30).

It is hardly surprising that the prophets are often dismissed as pessimists. Their warnings were largely unheeded, so the emphasis on coming judgment increased. False prophets, who got their 'prophecies' from each other (see Jeremiah ch. 23) were optimistic about the future and ridiculed those who spoke of 'doom and gloom'.

Yet this is a misleading impression. If the prophets expressed immediate despair, they also conveyed ultimate hope. They believed in a God who keeps his promises, never breaks his covenants and will not let his people go.

Beyond the retribution lay restoration. The next sentence in Nehemiah's prayer picks this up: 'But in your great mercy you did not put an end to them, or abandon them, for you are a gracious and merciful God' (Neh. 9:31).

The essence of prophetic promise for the future was that God would intervene in human history and re-establish his rule on earth, destroying the wicked and vindicating the righteous. Later, this expectancy was condensed into the simple phrase 'the kingdom of God', which the Jews longed to see established on earth as it is in heaven. We must now consider the relevance of this concept to baptism in the Spirit.

THE KINGDOM OF GOD

There is a profound connection between the Spirit and this 'kingdom' (better translated as 'kingship' or 'reign', for it is more concerned with rule than realm, with power than place). We have already seen that the Spirit executed the heavenly commands on earth in creation. The same is true of redemption. The reign of God is demonstrated wherever the Spirit is active.

The prophets therefore spoke of a time when the Spirit would come in greater power than ever before. But his work in human beings would become narrower before it became broader. His power would be concentrated in one person before being distributed to many. The kingdom would come first in a Spirit-anointed sovereign, then through Spirit-saturated subjects.

Spirit-anointed sovereign Jewish hopes had a human as well as a divine dimension. They looked for a restoration of the Davidic dynasty. Though many limited his reign to national boundaries, some had grasped the prophetic note of universal sovereignty over all the nations and to the ends of the earth (sounded strongly in Isaiah 40-66).

He would be qualified for this awesome task by the Spirit. As David had been the only king with whom the Spirit continued to work (1 Sam. 16:13; his greatest fear was to lose the Spirit – Ps. 51:11), so the same would be true of this 'son of David'. Three prophecies in Isaiah describe this anointing in greater detail.

Isaiah 11:1-2 He is called 'a shoot from the stump of Jesse', that is from the same roots as the tree which had been cut down. 'The Spirit of the LORD [Yahweh] will rest [remain, reside, stay] on him – the Spirit of wisdom and of understanding, the Spirit of counsel and of power, the Spirit of knowledge and of the fear of the LORD [Yahweh].' All these are qualifications to rule a people wisely and well. The prophecy goes on to describe his absolutely fair judgments, particularly on behalf of those who cannot defend themselves.

Isaiah 42:1-3 This expands on the Spirit's enabling him to bring justice world-wide. As we know, justice is the only foundation for lasting peace. In particular he will show sensitivity to those who have been hurt and suppressed and pursue his task with patience and persistence (Matthew 12:18-21 applies this scripture to Jesus after he had healed *all* the sick brought to him).

Isaiah 61:1-3 This promise focuses on his mission and its results. Through the Spirit he will bring good news to the poor and the sad, release for the captured and imprisoned. This 'anointed' deliverer will proclaim the inauguration of God's 'favour', a promise reminiscent of the fiftieth year of 'jubilee' (see Leviticus 25). How significant that Jesus was given the scroll of Isaiah to preach from for his very first sermon, in his home town of Nazareth – and that he opened it at this very passage (Luke 4:16-19; though he deliberately omitted its final words, 'and the day of vengeance of our God').

This anointing would be comprehensive, permanent and unlimited. He would combine the roles of prophet, priest and king. All the gifts and graces of the Spirit would be his. He would be perfectly capable of doing, being and saying whatever God wanted. Such would be the narrowing down of the Spirit, in one man.

But what sort of a kingdom can a good king, even a perfect king, have if his subjects are bad? As a good king lives for the welfare of his subjects, good subjects are needed who seek to do the will of the king. Conversely, a bad king is only concerned for himself, his own power, wealth or status, and bad subjects for their own pleasure and desires.

Spirit-saturated subjects In approaching this aspect of prophetic promise for the future it will be helpful to consider the limits of the past.

The coming of the Spirit on anyone was always a conscious experience with audible and visible evidence.

Something definitely happened. But it was neither common nor continuous.

On the one hand, only a comparatively small number experienced such an event, perhaps about one hundred and fifty in all, scattered over two thousand years of Israel's history. The patriarchs, judges, kings and prophets together would not be a large company. The vast majority were not touched. It may or may not be significant that, though women prophesied, the Spirit is only mentioned in connection with men, perhaps because leadership was male. Though millions benefited from the few who were 'anointed', there is no mention of any desire for or reception of this anointing on the part of the ordinary average Israelite. It was enough that their leaders were thus qualified.

On the other hand, even for the few who did enjoy such an anointing, it was not necessarily a lasting experience. The divine touch could be intermittent, fleeting and could even be withdrawn altogether. Samson is the classic example (Judg. 16:20). King Saul is another, though even after the Spirit of the Lord (*ruach adonai*) departed and an evil spirit took over, he still 'prophesied' (1 Sam. 18:10; we are not told whether the words he was singing to the accompaniment of David's harp were of divine origin – probably not, since the Spirit had already departed from him).

Of a few we are told that 'the Spirit *is* in them', which contains more than a hint of an ongoing relationship. Such are Joseph (Gen. 41:38), Moses (Num. 11:17), Joshua (Num. 27:16), Samuel, Elijah, Elisha and Daniel.

Most, if not all, of these could be considered as 'types' (foreshadowings) of Christ. Of one man alone, David, is it specifically stated that he received the Spirit and the Spirit remained with him 'from that day forward' (1 Sam. 16:13); he was the supreme type of Christ, with his unique combination of spiritual gifts.

All this was to change quite radically when the kingdom of God came, according to the prophets. Moses' desire to see *all* the Lord's people prophesying as a sign of having the Spirit 'put on' them (Num. 11:29), rather than just the official institutional leaders jealous for their monopoly, was picked up by a number of prophets who promised in the name of the Lord that one day this would come about.

Joel was the first to do so (and is probably the best known through being quoted in Peter's preaching on the day of Pentecost). The Lord would pour out his Spirit on 'all flesh' (2:28) – not every human being, but all God's people and all kinds within that people, regardless of age, sex or class, as he goes on to make clear. Old and young, men and women, master and servant, would alike receive this outpouring (note the *liquid* metaphor, later used in the New Testament to describe baptism in Spirit). The immediate result would be that they would all *prophesy*, speaking words given by God. They would therefore receive revelation as well as give it, sometimes in pictures as well as words – visions while awake (for the active young) and dreams while asleep (for the sedentary aged!). The ultimate result would be that many would call on the name of the Lord and be saved. Joel may have been the first to predict this amazing possibility, but he was not the last.

Isaiah followed with more details. He put particular emphasis on the fact that this would not happen in the lives of his contemporaries, but to their 'offspring' and 'descendants' (44:33-5). Instead of being embarrassed, they will be unashamed to identify themselves with the Lord and his people, proud to belong to both and boldly witnessing to it (both this and the preceding chapter emphasise their calling to be 'witnesses' to Jahweh; 43:10, 12; 44:8 – verses from which the cult of Jehovah's Witnesses took its name). Before leaving the passage, it is important to notice again the use of *liquid* metaphors for the Spirit: 'I will pour water on the thirsty land, and streams on the dry ground.' The result of the outpouring in speech is further emphasised in a later prophecy, worth quoting in full: '"As for me, this is my covenant with them," says the Lord. "My Spirit, who is on you, and my words that I have put in your mouth will not depart from your mouth, or from the mouths of your children, or from the mouths of their descendants from this time on and for ever," says the Lord' (59:21). The fourfold mention of mouths makes it quite clear that a primary purpose of giving the Spirit is to enable people to prophesy, to speak out words put in their mouths by God. Notice also that this is part of a 'covenant' between God and his people.

Jeremiah is noteworthy for his promise of a 'new covenant' between Yahweh and Israel, in which God will forgive and forget their sins – which will deal with their past – writing his laws inside them on mind and heart rather than outside them on tablets of stone – which will secure their future (31:31-4). This is later expanded: 'I will give them singleness of heart and action . . . so that they will never turn away from me' (32:39-40). Of course, Jeremiah tells us *what* this new covenant will do, but not *how* it will be done. He does not specifically mention the Spirit, though the word 'inspire' (inbreathe) gives a strong hint. That it will be brought about by the Spirit becomes very clear when we listen to another prophet.

Ezekiel picks up the inward application of Jeremiah's 'new covenant': 'I will give them an undivided heart and put a new spirit in them; I will remove from them their heart of stone and give them a heart of flesh [i.e. soft and sensitive rather than hard and stubborn]. Then they will follow my decrees and be careful to keep my laws' (11:19-20). The phrase 'a new spirit' is ambiguous; it could be both human and divine, probably the former in this context. However, in later statements about the same transformation, Ezekiel makes it crystal clear that it is the result of the Spirit's coming. 'I will give you a new heart and put a new spirit in you . . . And I will put my Spirit in you and move you to follow my decrees' (36:26-7). The presence of the divine Spirit will change the human spirit. Later still, Ezekiel sounds just like

Joel: 'I will no longer hide my face from them, for I will pour out my Spirit on the house of Israel, declares the sovereign LORD' (39:29; the 'liquid' Spirit again). Both Jeremiah and Ezekiel stress the moral renewal that will result from this outpouring, the inward silent obedience rather than the outward spoken testimony. But these are not in opposition to one another, much less contradiction. Both will result from the anointing. Power and purity belong together. Either without the other is ineffective. The world must see and hear the mighty works of God. Lips and lives must give a consistent testimony. Human nature is prone to want the power rather than the purity, but the Spirit wants to give both – together.

It is time to draw the threads of this chapter together. I doubt if any reader now feels it has been a waste of time to study the Old Testament in order to understand baptism in the Spirit. Indeed, a knowledge of this Jewish background is essential, as it is for almost everything in the New Testament. A few concluding remarks are in order.

We have said little about other 'spirits' which can activate behaviour and influence character. Human beings can be 'possessed' by evil and unclean spirits. The Jews knew about spirits of adultery, jealousy, deception, fear, confusion and depression. They are particularly associated with mediums, spiritism and occult practices. A marked characteristic of those afflicted is that their behaviour is uncontrolled by themselves and uncontrollable by others. They are overpowered by bad spirits.

However, all are still under the overall sovereignty of God, as is Satan (read Job 1). They cannot inflict damage without God's permission. He can and does use them in discipline – for example, sending lying spirits into false prophets, not called by him, sowing confusion in the minds of his people's enemies.

His own Spirit is in marked contrast. Though strong, the power is not overwhelming. It requires co-operation. The Spirit may be 'grieved' by unco-operative wills (Isa. 63:10). Human beings are free to 'resist', refusing the aid and guidance offered. The possibility of his departure is very real.

It is pertinent to consider the Apocrypha at this point, that collection of books covering the four hundred years of Israel's history between the last prophet, Malachi, and the events recorded by Matthew, the first book in the New Testament. These writings should not be included in any Bible, for a very good reason. The Spirit was not directly active among them during that time. There were no messages from God, no 'thus says the Lord', no prophets and no prophecies. Neither were there any miracles. Their leaders, whether religious or political, were left to their own ingenuity and resources. Occasionally, their struggles for independence were successful, as under the Maccabees, but only for a short time.

They could only hope, long and pray for the kingdom of God to appear and take over. Then the Spirit would be poured out, not just on the leaders but on the entire nation. How powerful a people they would then be. Few considered how pure they would need to be as well.

It would be a long wait. Yet the hopes were kept alive, passed down from generation to generation. When would the kingdom of God break in? When would 'the king of the Jews' be born? (They knew where – Bethlehem, the city of David.) When would the Spirit be poured out? And how would these three hopes be related to each other? They learned to live with these unanswered questions, for four hundred years.

Then a baby boy was born, in a context of divine miracles and messages. After thirty years of obscurity, as a refugee in Egypt and a carpenter in Nazareth, he emerged in public, but only after his cousin John, adopting the diet and dress of Elijah (and thus fulfilling the last prophecy centuries before, Malachi 4:5), had announced his imminent arrival and urged moral and spiritual cleansing in preparation. The emphasis would be on purity rather than power, the one being a necessary prerequisite for the other.

John is the bridge between the old and the new. In a very real sense, he was the last Old Testament prophet (Matt. 11:11). After waiting so long to hear from God, it is not at all surprising that the nation flocked to hear him speak. That he told them they were not ready, not clean enough, for what was about to happen was the surprise, and his method of correcting this situation – plunging them into a muddy river – was even more so.

But he was the forerunner of the new era about to dawn, the promised new covenant, the kingdom at hand, almost within their reach and grasp. The one who would pour out the Spirit, plunge them into the flood, was already among them.

3

The Final Fulfilment

'The New is in the Old concealed; the Old is in the New revealed.' The cliché is a useful summary of the relationship between the two Testaments which together make up our Bible.

We have already seen how many hints of and pointers to 'baptism in the Spirit' can be found in the Jewish scriptures, though the phrase itself is not there. Yet without this background, it would have made no sense to John's listeners at all. They may not have understood its full implications, but they would have had a pretty good idea of what it would do for them.

The Christian scriptures make explicit what was already implicit in the Jewish. Both the phrase and its meaning are clearly spelled out in the apostolic writings. However, before looking into these, one or two ground rules need to be laid down.

The most important is that we shall not limit our study to those verses and passages which contain the exact wording, 'baptised in Spirit'. There are seven of these – four in the Gospels (Matt. 3:11; Mark 1:8; Luke 3:16; John 1:33; all these, of course, are separate accounts of the same occasion, John's preaching), two in Acts (1:5 on the lips of Jesus and 11:16 spoken by Peter), one in the Epistles (1 Cor. 12:13; used by Paul). An examination of these few texts would be fairly short and quite straightforward. But our task is not as simple as that.

The reason is that a careful reading reveals a considerable number of synonyms for 'baptised' when describing the same happening. The Gospels use 'come', 'clothed with', 'gift' and 'promise'. Acts uses 'fall upon', 'come upon', 'poured out upon', 'gift', 'promise' and 'filled'. The Epistles use 'given', 'sealed', 'anointed' and 'deposit'.

But there is one synonym used in the Gospels, Acts and the Epistles whose significance cannot be exaggerated: namely the word 'received'. To be 'baptised in Spirit' is the same thing as to 'receive the Spirit'. To 'receive the Spirit' is the same thing as being 'baptised in Spirit'.

This equation has profound theological implications. Any attempt to develop a doctrine of Spirit baptism must start here. To anticipate what is later explained in this book, the failure to identify 'baptised' with 'received' has led to the differences and even divisions between 'pentecostals' and 'evangelicals', without which a book like this need never have been written (the next two chapters will spell this out).

So our examination of relevant New Testament data must include passages containing all these synonyms and give particular attention to 'receive'.

There is another guideline which will have a considerable effect on our conclusions.

It has become customary to analyse the relevant passages by authorship, taking each author's contribution as a separate entity. What does Luke say about this? What does Paul say? Or John? This approach produces a number of different 'theologies' from one Testament: Lukan, Pauline or Johannine. Or, in the present case, different 'pneumatologies' (the label given to that branch of theology studying the 'Spirit' – the Greek word for which is *pneuma*).

This approach can be helpful. Biblical writers were not just word processors. Revelation came through their different temperaments and experiences, giving them a variety of approach and insight. Their contributions are not characterised by uniformity, but there is a unity in spite of the diversity. This method becomes harmful when taken to an extreme and used to try and prove disagreement rather than diversity, contradiction rather than complementarity. Authors are set over against rather than alongside each other. The differences are exaggerated to the point of division. Certainly they should be allowed to speak for themselves, without one being forced into the vocabulary and thought forms of another. But to polarise them by contrast rather than comparison is to create imaginary conflicts with inadequate evidence.

The danger is then that Bible students are faced with choices which scripture itself does not demand. Whose theology do you believe and live by? 'Paul?' 'John?' 'No, just Jesus.' (That last answer is just as bad as the others, according to 1 Cor. 1:12-13!). Such partisanship is utterly alien to the New Testament. It creates 'a canon within the canon'. The word 'canon', from Latin and Greek, means 'rule'. When applied to scripture it means that the *whole* of it provides the rule or standard measurement of all matters in belief and behaviour. When part of it is set against another part, especially when one part is used to neutralise or negate another, that is an improper use of the whole 'canon of scripture'.

Alas, this abuse has been very obvious in the subject before us. Luke and Paul have been treated in this way, in spite of being travelling companions on the same missionary team. The way some scholars talk, they must have spent most of their time arguing about how, when and why the Holy Spirit is received! We are told that for Luke this was a subsequent and sensational experience of power for mission, whereas for Paul it was an initial element in salvation of which the recipient may be unaware. 'Pentecostals' want to follow the former and 'evangelicals' the latter.

A more subtle form of this false dichotomy is to draw a contrast between their writings. On the one side are those who base all their doctrine on Acts and the Gospel of Luke as records of the Spirit's actual activity. On the other side are those who say that doctrine cannot be established on the basis of the 'narrative' portions of scripture (that means most of the Bible!), but can only be drawn from the 'didactic' (i.e. teaching) parts, like the Epistles. Once again, we are faced with an 'either/ or'. Why can't it be 'both/and'? Only when the narrated Scriptures of Luke and the didactic Scriptures of Paul are taken equally seriously and in their own right are we likely to see a true union of pentecostal and evangelical insights. Both parties expound those parts of scripture which agree with their teaching and try to explain away those which don't. Prejudice has a lot to answer for!

In this book I shall be synthetic rather then analytic, putting the different insights together rather than pulling them apart. Starting from the assumption that the Holy Spirit himself inspired all the writers and all the writings in the New Testament, we shall seek the *whole* picture of baptism in the Spirit, made up of all the available data, regardless of who was used to communicate any part of it.

However, some sort of analysis is necessary to bring the parts into focus. The wood is made up of trees, and both must be observed. Some can't see the wood for the trees, but others can't see the trees for the wood! It is necessary to classify the trees to describe the nature of the wood.

How, then, shall we group the New Testament material, if not by author? I am going to use a simpler and, I believe, more helpful classification, following a chronological pattern – before, during and after. This has the additional advantage of following the 'genre' (kind or style of literature). Let me explain.

All the Gospel references are in the future tense, something that *will happen* after the time covered in them. Acts talks about something that *is happening*; it is written 'on location'. The Epistles look back to something that *has happened* ('you were baptised in one Spirit'). Note that the remaining book, Revelation, contains no relevant references. This arrangement of the material highlights one very pertinent fact. The references in the Gospels looking forward and those in the Epistles looking back are devoid of any description, much less a definition, of what 'baptism in Spirit' actually *is*. The Gospels are concerned with *when* it will happen and the Epistles with *why* it has happened, but only Acts tells us *how* it happens. The truth is that without Acts we simply wouldn't know what 'baptism in Spirit' is. It is only anticipated in the Gospels and assumed in the Epistles, but it is articulated (through recorded experiences of it) in Acts. Foresight in the Gospels and hindsight in the Epistles are no substitute for the insight in Acts. We can now see why some have been eager to exclude Acts from consideration. That leaves anyone free to supply their own opinion about what constitutes such a baptism and, in particular, the liberty to deny that an identifiable experience is an essential element. The motives behind this are usually practical and will be dealt with in detail later (Chapter 7).

The different emphases of the writers and the varied perspectives in the Gospels, Acts and the Epistles must all be included and reconciled if a balanced and biblical understanding is to be gained. With this guideline firmly in mind, we are ready to study 'baptism in Spirit' (and its synonyms) in the New Testament, starting with the Gospel references looking forward to it.

THE GOSPELS – BEFORE

'Baptism in Spirit' is mentioned in all four Gospels. Granted, all four references relate to the same event, John's ministry by the Jordan, but the repetition is nevertheless highly significant. Why should such prominence be given to this single statement from John's preaching (Mark 1:7 indicates that this was a constant feature in his message)? This emphasis is appreciated all the more when compared with what else is included in all four Gospels and, even more, with what is not.

Actually, very little is common to Matthew, Mark, Luke and John. The death, burial and resurrection of Jesus are portrayed in great detail by all four writers. But that is the fundamental heart of the gospel, as Paul would later teach (1 Cor. 15:3-4). The need for faith as a response is also prominent in all four. For the rest, there is remarkably little shared material.

Jesus' conception and birth, his exile and boyhood, his baptism and temptation, Peter's confession and the subsequent transfiguration, the last supper and agony in Gethsemane – none of these are found in all four Gospels. Neither are all but one of his miracles (the feeding of the five thousand) nor any of his teaching, even the parables for which he was so well known. His famous 'I am' claims are in only one.

Yet all four Gospels begin with John's practice of baptising in water and highlight the single promise that the one coming after him would be powerful enough to baptise in Spirit. This cannot be coincidental.

The repetition is more impressive when we consider the readers addressed by the Gospel writers. Mark and Luke were written for unbelievers (the latter for just one such). Matthew was written for 'new' believers, mostly Jewish (the five blocks of teaching on the lifestyle, mission, growth, community and future of the kingdom are all addressed to those already sons and subjects). John was written to 'old' believers, urging them to go on believing in the full humanity and divinity of Jesus and thus go on having eternal life (3:16 and 20:31 use the present continuous tense for both verbs). All need to hear about or be reminded of water and Spirit baptism.

The dating of the Gospels is also relevant. Most, if not all, were probably written after the book of Acts and certainly after the events recorded there. If, as some would have it, Pentecost was the one and only fulfilment of John the baptiser's prediction, why should the Gospel writers emphasise it without explaining this? Their readers could so easily assume that the promise had a continual application.

One can only conclude that all four Gospels give such prominence to water and Spirit baptism because that is how the discipleship of everyone who responds to the gospel of the death, burial and resurrection of Jesus actually starts. That is the beginning of the gospel for them existentially, as it was historically, when John prepared the way.

It is therefore passing strange that so many evangelists today preach a 'gospel' that includes neither water nor Spirit baptism. They don't hesitate to preach 'repentance' or the need to be 'born again', though neither of these is in all four Gospels. Yet they shrink from quoting John's ringing affirmation: 'He will baptise you in Holy Spirit'.

But we are jumping ahead (a bad habit of preachers!). We must continue to look into the Gospels, separately now because of slight variation between John and the Synoptics (the word means 'to view together' and is used of Matthew, Mark and Luke because of the similarity of content).

Synoptics The first thing to do is to dissect the phrase itself, then look at its immediate and its wider context. While there is neither a description nor a definition, we may nevertheless learn a great deal from the statement, 'He will baptise you in holy Spirit' (Matt. 3:11; Mark 1:8; Luke 3:16).

The verb is the best place to start. 'Baptise' is always used, never the noun 'baptism', though that is used when linked with water (Mark 7:4; Heb. 6:2; 9:10). Two deductions may be made. First, verbs are more dynamic than nouns. They describe an action rather than an article, an event rather than an object. Compare 'Did you get the baptism?' with 'Were you baptised?' and the difference is readily apparent. Second, a verb has to have a subject and therefore draws attention to the person performing the action (in this case, 'he'), which the noun does not. It is unfortunate that in much discussion today the noun has replaced the verb. Indeed, I have been using it already. The title of my book is rather cumbersome because I wanted to draw attention both to the verb and to its subject.

The meaning of the verb has been touched on earlier. The Greek (*baptizo*) is rarely translated; it is usually simply transliterated into English letters, which hides its true significance. It is an intensive form of 'dip' (*bapto*), and was used of dipping a bucket in a well or a cup into a bowl of wine, soaking wool or cloth in a pan of dye, or even of a ship sunk at sea (we would probably think of a 'baptised' ship as being launched, much as we launch babies into life!). In other words, it means to 'plunge' a solid into a liquid so that it is completely covered ('drench' would be another English equivalent). It can be used for washing hands or dishes (e.g. Luke 11:38), but that is because they are also completely covered by water even if it is just poured over them. It cannot possibly be used for sprinkling. That John the plunger immersed rather than poured is confirmed by his choice of site 'because there was plenty of water' (John 3:23). Jesus himself 'went up out of the water' (Matt. 3:16). There are some curious ancient paintings which portray John immersing the lower half of the body but sprinkling the top half, which may indicate the later transition to a radically different mode! But few scholars would maintain any other meaning for the biblical usage than 'submerged in' or 'completely covered by'. That this is the same connotation when applied to 'Spirit' goes without saying, especially since John made the comparison with 'water' in the same sentence. The contrast is in the medium, not the action.

Two more features of the verb need to be pointed out. It is in the future tense: 'will baptise'. It was not happening already; indeed, it could not. Another three years would pass before it began to happen. As we have already noted, there is not one reference in the Gospels to anyone being baptised in Spirit (see below for John 20:22 as a remotely possible exception). The verb is active ('will baptise you'), not passive ('you will be baptised', though this is the form in Acts and the Epistles). Once again, John is drawing attention to the activator rather than the action, the person rather than the plunge, the one who will give this baptism rather than the many who will receive it.

Of course, when John began saying this, he had no idea *who* the subject ('he') really was, only *what* he was – the coming king, the Messiah, bringing the kingdom of God back to earth and for whom John was preparing the way. The Synoptic Gospels are faithfully recording his preaching before he was able to put a name to this profile, a pointer to their historical accuracy. He only knew him as the 'One' who would wield greater power and would be worthy of far greater honour.

The object of the verb is 'you', which is addressed to all John's hearers. They would have a second 'baptism', though not at his hands. This is a promise that is both corporate (all of 'you') and individual (each of 'you'). It is of unlimited application (not just 'one hundred and twenty of you'!). It was said to everyone who came to John for his baptism of repentance and forgiveness after confession (note that this would not include children under twelve, much less babies). They all needed it and they would all be able to have it. The promise was made to the general public, not a select few.

Prepositions are important. The verb 'baptise' is always followed by 'in' (Greek *en*), which relates to the medium in which an object or a person is plunged (a noun in the dative case follows the preposition, in this context 'water', *hudati*, and 'Spirit', *pneumati*). Again, there is a cover-up in English translations where the preposition is frequently given its less usual meaning of 'with' or 'by', effectively suppressing questions about modern methods of 'baptising'. Clearly, 'in' is the appropriate word to use of John's water baptism, and his own analogy demands the same for Spirit baptism.

So what is the medium in the latter case? Yet again, the English translators have misled us – by inserting the definite article ('the'), which is not in the Greek. Its addition radically alters the sense of John's statement. To understand how, we must return to our Old Testament study.

We have already seen that the adjective 'holy' was rarely applied to the Spirit of God – in fact, only three times and then in contrast to the sinful spirit of men (Ps. 51:11; Isa. 63:10-11). Even in these, the definite article is not used – only 'your holy Spirit' or 'his holy spirit', never 'the Holy Spirit'. The significance of this is that *they did not then understand that the Spirit was a person as well as a power*. 'The Spirit of God' was God's own breath, his invisible force, not a distinct person within the Godhead, as later revelation would make clear. The term covered a divine attribute and actions, more impersonal than personal. The 'Spirit' was something rather than someone, an 'it' rather than a 'he'.

Christians, enjoying the fuller revelation in Jesus, think of 'the Holy Spirit' as a person. They see a title, even a name, in the phrase, invariably using the definite article to indicate this. But it is very doubtful if John had this understanding. He was preaching long before Jesus made it clear that the Spirit was another divine person like himself.

He might, had he used English, have spelled 'Spirit' with a capital 'S', to show he was talking about the divine and not the human spirit. But he would spell 'holy' with a small 'h' as a qualifying adjective, not a proper name. Our Bibles should say: 'he will baptise you in holy Spirit'.

This puts far more emphasis on the word 'holy' and puts the whole statement into its proper context. Remember, John could help people to get their past forgiven but could not help them to keep the future free from sin. He could get them clean, but not keep them clean. Against this background his promise makes so much more sense – 'he will baptise you in *holy* Spirit', which would meet the very need John could not meet. (We could re-translate this as 'drench you in holy power' or even 'in power to be holy'.)

When Christians read '*the* Holy Spirit' in their Bibles they think of the person rather than of his holiness. It then becomes possible to divorce the purity from the power and see 'baptism in Spirit' solely in terms of service to others and not related to one's own sanctification. Pentecostal doctrine has been particularly prone to this misunderstanding as we shall see (in Chapter 5). It is, of course, both. Purity and power are twin results. Now one and now the other is given primary attention. But there can be little doubt that John's emphasis was on moral cleansing. This is confirmed by an intriguing additional phrase recorded by Matthew: 'and with fire' (Matt. 3:11). There are at least three interpretations of this 'fiery' baptism.

First, popular preaching has often interpreted it as *zeal* or enthusiasm. Spirit baptism is said to set people 'on fire for the Lord'. Appeal is made to the 'tongues of fire' touching the heads of those who were present at Pentecost (Acts 2:3) and their subsequent boldness in evangelism. By derivation it is also applied to seasons of revival (when, in some cases, actual flames have been seen on church or chapel roofs). Though it makes for impressive rhetoric, there is some doubt whether this was the original meaning.

Second, the 'fire' has been seen as a *purging* agent, refining what is less than pure by burning out the dross (as in the production of gold or silver). Baptism in 'holy Spirit and fire' would thus achieve the negative result of removing what is not 'holy' as well as the positive filling with what is holy. There may be some truth in this, but there is a far more likely interpretation.

Third, 'fire' is a symbol of *punishment*, of judgment, of destruction. God is a 'consuming fire' in both the Old and the New Testaments (Deut. 4:24; Heb. 12:29). He uses fire, not so much to refine the righteous, but to destroy the wicked. In the prophecy of Malachi we find the warning that 'the day' will again 'see the distinction between the righteous and the wicked, between those who serve God and those who do not' (Mal. 3:18). In the Hebrew text there is no division between this and what we call Chapter 4. The prophet went on to say: 'Surely the day is coming; it will burn like a furnace. All the arrogant and every evildoer will be stubble, and that day that is coming will set them on fire . . . Not a root or a branch will be left to them . . . they will be ashes under the soles of your feet' (Mal. 4:1-3). Then he added: 'See, I will send you the prophet Elijah before that great and dreadful day of the Lord comes' (Mal. 4:5).

It cannot be a coincidence that John echoed so much of this prophecy, particularly the bonfires that conclude every harvest-time. Only two or three pages in our Bibles have to be turned to reach his message: '. . . and with fire. His winnowing fork is in his hand, and he will clear his threshing floor, gathering wheat into the barn and burning up the chaff with unquenchable fire' (Matt. 3:11-12); that last phrase was picked up later by Jesus himself as a description of hell. Note the separation between the useful wheat and the useless chaff before the fire is started.

It seems clear that John was referring to one baptiser but two quite different baptisms, for two separate groups of people, depending on how ready they were for 'that day'. Those who had cleaned up their lives as far as they could would be baptised in holy Spirit; those who had not would be baptised in destructive fire. Such a message would give great urgency to the need for repentance and baptism. It is not surprising that so many responded. Only those who considered themselves clean enough failed to respond: 'All the people, even the tax collectors . . . had been baptised by John. But the Pharisees and experts in the law rejected God's purpose for themselves, because they had not been baptised by John' (Luke 7:29-30).

But the baptism 'in fire' never materialised. The wicked were *not* burned up. The Pharisees and scribes continued in their hypocrisy. The Sadducees continued in their corrupt priesthood. The Romans continued their cruel occupation. No fire of judgment descended. Much later, John, already imprisoned for his public denunciation of Herod's immoral and illegal marriage, sent an anxious enquiry to Jesus: 'Are you the one who was to come, or should we expect someone else?' (Luke 7:20). It was an added burden to his sufferings that he feared he had been involved in a case of mistaken identity and seriously misled his public. Had he named the wrong person as the Messiah, a very serious error to have made? Jesus' reply, quoting a number of Isaiah's prophecies (Isa. 29:18-19; 35:5-6; 61:1-2), may not have fully settled John's doubts. Many good things were happening but nothing was being done about bad people. Where was the baptism in fire? Or, for that matter, the baptism in holy Spirit? Why was Jesus not fulfilling John's prophecy?

The solution to this dilemma is again to be found in the Old Testament and the incomplete revelation given to the prophets. They were given many details about the coming 'day of the Lord' and could be forgiven for concluding that everything would at least happen close together, if not strictly within the same twenty-four hours. What they could not have understood through their telescopic vision of the future 'peaks' of history was that there could be long 'valleys' of time between them, that God's 'day' would be phased, his kingdom re-established on earth in stages. In particular, they were not told that this would be accomplished over *two comings* of the king Messiah, not one. He would come first for the purpose of redemption, and only later for retribution, first to bring holiness to those who would receive and later to deal with those who refused.

Christians, living between the two comings, understand this very well, but to John and the Jews of his day it would have been a novel and radical concept. This explains both John's disappointment with Jesus and the Jews' disappointment with him, leading to his execution for making false claims. They did not realise that they needed to have their sin taken away, as did the whole world. Nor did they grasp that his first coming would be limited to seeking and saving the lost. Above all, they could not have seen that his death would be the means of their salvation, though Isaiah had predicted that God's Spirit-anointed servant would be pierced for their transgressions, crushed for their iniquities and have the iniquity of them all laid on him (Isa. 53:5-6).

The baptism of fire will come on the day of judgment, but did come on Jesus himself, the one person who did not warrant it, and on no one else. How meaningful his anguished words now become: 'I have come to bring *fire* on the earth, and how I wish it were already kindled! But I have a *baptism* to undergo, and how distressed I am until it is completed!' (Luke 12:49-50). With these words he seems to point to a link between the beginning and end of his public ministry, as if the one involved the other, his first baptism inevitably leading to the second. We must now return to the first.

The climax of John's ministry was to baptise his cousin Jesus. This is an essential part of the wider context of John's statement which links the two baptisms in water and Spirit. These two elements were also closely associated in Jesus' experience, which would later become a pattern for Christian initiation.

As is well known, John was extremely reluctant to baptise his cousin, suggesting that it should be the other way round (revealing, incidentally, that he was not himself baptised!). The grounds for his hesitation were quite simple. Jesus was already living a clean and holy life. Had John heard this from a human or divine source? Whatever, Jesus insisted on being treated like everybody else, giving as his reason: 'It is proper for us to do this to fulfil all righteousness' (Matt. 3:15). It is always right to do what is right, to obey God's commands. This action, by the one person who did not need it, removes all excuses from those who refuse to follow him.

If Jesus did not need to be baptised in water, neither did he need to be baptised in *holy* Spirit. Nevertheless, the Spirit came upon him in a form that was visible to himself and others: a 'dove' (compare the brooding hovering Spirit in Gen. 1:2). It is important to notice that this did not happen while he was being baptised but *after* he came up out of the water and as he was *praying* (Matt. 3:16; Luke 3:21-2). This sequence reappears in Acts and could be regarded as the norm for disciples of Christ.

There is a significant change in language when this reception of 'the Spirit' is described. The definite article is now used, though it is doubtful if even yet this indicates understanding of a person. This is the language of the Old Testament again: *the* Spirit of God (see Matt. 3:16) as an observed object rather than a personal encounter, seen as a bird rather than a being. More importantly, 'holy' is not used, nor is Jesus said to be 'plunged in holy'. He did not need any more purity than he had already. But 'the Spirit' points to an endowment with supernatural ability. In his genuine humanity, even the Son of God needed this to fulfil his mission, both to proclaim the message (to be '*the* prophet') and to perform miracles. Years later, Peter was to refer to this event in this way: 'how God anointed Jesus of Nazareth with Holy Spirit [by this time the name of a divine person] and power, and how he went around doing good and healing all who were under the power of the devil, because God was with him' (Acts 10:38). Matthew confirms that it was by the power of the Spirit that Jesus cast out demons (Matt. 12:28). To deny this was unforgivable blasphemy (Matt. 12:32).

Jesus also received guidance from the Spirit, leading him into the wilderness where he was alone (Matt. 4:1; Luke 4:1; Mark 1:12 has 'driving'!), then from this solitary time back to the crowds in Galilee.

This 'anointing' qualified Jesus for two titles: *Mashiach*

in Hebrew and *Christus* in Greek. Both have tended to lose their connection with the Spirit, as later the word 'Christian' and even 'christening' would. They point to the reception of the Spirit.

There is one remaining verse in the Synoptic Gospels to be studied: 'If you then, though you are evil, know how to give good gifts to your children, how much more will your Father in heaven give holy Spirit to those who go on asking him!' (Luke 11:13). There is no definite article before 'holy Spirit'; it is the same phrase as John's. Certainly, it does not use 'baptised', but 'give' is used, the other side of receiving. The verb 'ask' is in the present continuous tense and should be translated accordingly, as in our quotation; this is amply borne out by the preceding parable, in which a man goes on knocking at a neighbour's door at midnight until he gets up and gives him what he needs.

Jesus encourages such persistent prayer with the promise: 'So I say to you: Go on asking and it will be given you; go on seeking and you will find; go on knocking and the door will be opened to you' (Luke 11:9).

We need to ask who this counsel is intended for. Surely not unbelievers (we shall find in John's Gospel that the world cannot 'receive' the Spirit). But if believers automatically received the Spirit as soon as they believed, they wouldn't need to ask for this 'gift'. Actually, we shall find in Acts that believing in Jesus and receiving the Spirit are two different things. It is the right of every believer to be given the Spirit. He comes in answer to prayer, as he did on Jesus and later many others (Acts 8:15, for example). The gift is to be had for the asking, persisted in until the Spirit is given and received.

At the end of his first volume, Dr Luke provides a link to his second by quoting from the last commands and promises of Jesus. The disciples are to be his 'witnesses', carrying the message of repentance and forgiveness to all nations. But they must first be equipped for the task. So he tells them to 'stay in the city [Jerusalem] until you have been clothed with power from on high' (Luke 24:47-9). The second volume makes it clear that this is a reference to baptism in Spirit (Acts 1:4-5). Whereas John had focused on purity for themselves as the result, Jesus now highlights power for others. That is because the context is now the universal mission for which he has been preparing them. Note that the 'power' is still not available to them. They would have to 'wait' nearly two more months for it. That is because the power would come 'from on high', but Jesus was not yet there and he was the baptiser in Spirit. Only after he had returned to heaven could he 'clothe' (cover, envelop) them in the power (Spirit) of God. Without this their witness would be weak and their evangelism would not be very effective.

The addition to Mark's Gospel (16:9-20), replacing the original 'lost ending', also highlights supernatural power to drive out demons, speak in new languages, pick up snakes and drink poison safely, and heal the sick. Such 'signs' later accompanied and endorsed the apostolic preaching.

This concludes our study of the relevant material in the Synoptic Gospels and we can now turn to John, where there is much more about the Holy Spirit.

John Written later than the others, John's Gospel contains far more material about the Holy Spirit, above all emphasising his person rather than his purity or power. We need to look into chapters 1, 3, 4, 7, 14, 15, 16 and 20.

Chapter 1 This begins with a unique prologue (1:1-18) declaring the eternity, personality, divinity and humanity of the 'Word' (Greek *logos*, which means 'the reason why', the '-ology' in every branch of science). This was the name John chose to give the pre-existent Son of God, before he became a man and was given the name 'Jesus'.

Then John the apostle, like the other Gospel writers, begins his narrative of Jesus' ministry with John the baptiser, again stressing both water and Spirit baptism. But there are some subtle and significant variations from the Synoptics.

Jesus' baptism in water is not mentioned, surprisingly. Yet this Gospel is the only one to tell us that Jesus, or rather his disciples, continued John's practice of baptising. For a time, both were doing the same thing a few miles apart in the River Jordan. Indeed, Jesus' followers were increasing in numbers while John's were decreasing, though Jesus soon moved away when people began to interpret this as rivalry (3:22-4:3).

Jesus' reception of the Spirit ('like a dove from heaven') is recorded. John had received a revelation from God that if he baptised many people, one of them would be given the Spirit visibly and this would identify the person for whom he was preparing the way. So getting the people cleaned up was not John's only purpose in baptising. He had an ulterior motive! He himself wanted to know, and he wanted everybody else to know, who the 'Coming One', the Messiah, would be. So he was ignorant about the name of the person he preached about when he began his ministry. 'I myself did not know him, but the reason I came baptising with water was that he might be revealed to Israel' (1:31).

He is not said to be surprised when it turned out to be his own cousin Jesus. Had his mother Elizabeth told him about their two miraculous conceptions, one in an old woman and one in a virgin, within six months of each other? One thing is certain, John had been fully aware of Jesus' flawless reputation (Matt. 3:14).

However, the major difference with the Synoptic record of the descent of the Spirit on Jesus is that the emphasis here is not what he received for himself, but what he would give to others. As John put it: 'The one who sent me to baptise in water [i.e. God] told me, "The man on whom you see the Spirit come down and remain is he who will baptise in holy Spirit"' (John 1:33). There are a number of points to be made here. Notice the presence of the definite article and the absence of 'holy' when talking about Jesus' reception of the Spirit (as in the Synoptics). The next thing to notice is that God himself, not John, coined the phrase 'baptise in holy Spirit' and called his Son 'the baptiser'. It is passing strange that so many Christians seem reluctant to use such language, originated as it was by God himself.

Above all, this passage contains the amazing claim that the same supernatural power enabling Jesus to proclaim his messages and perform his miracles would be made available to many others, by and through him. He receives this power to pass it on. It is because of this that he could later promise: 'I tell you the truth, anyone who has faith in me will do what I have been doing. He will do even greater things than these, because I am going to the Father' (14:12); note the link to his ascension, which would be expanded by Peter (Acts 2:33).

Chapter 3 Readers may be surprised that this passage, focusing on 'regeneration' (the new birth, being 'born again') should be included in a study of baptism in Spirit. The reason is quite simple. Many preachers and teachers have said that being born of the Spirit and being baptised in the Spirit are simultaneous events, even synonymous terms for one and the same thing. Are they right to make this identification? If they are, why are they so eager to use one term ('born of') and so reluctant to use the other ('baptised in')? There are some big questions here.

We need to remember that this chapter records a private conversation between Jesus and a Jewish theologian. 'Born again' terminology played no part in Jesus' public preaching or later in apostolic evangelism (nor should it in ours today; John's Gospel was directed to believers, as are the few other references to the new birth in the New Testament). We also need to note that Nicodemus was a Pharisee and as such would have refused to be baptised by John (Luke 7:30). His opening remark ('Rabbi, we know you are a teacher come from God. For no-one could perform the miraculous signs you are doing if God were not with him'; John 3:2) could be a veiled but odious comparison with John, who 'never performed a miraculous sign' (10:41).

Almost all scholars take verse 5 of chapter 3 as an expanded explanation of 'born again' in verse 3. The crux of the problem lies in the interpretation of the phrase: 'born of water and the Spirit', or, as the original Greek text has it, 'born out of water and Spirit' (the preposition is *ek*, which means 'out of', and there is no definite article). What does 'water' refer to and how does that relate to 'Spirit'?

Many tend to ignore the word 'water' altogether, emphasising the 'Spirit' only; but if pressed for an explanation they come up with a number of different opinions:

(i) 'Water' refers back to natural physical birth, preceded as it is by the 'breaking of the waters', the bag of liquid in which the foetus has floated in the mother's womb. Appeal is made to the mention of a womb by Nicodemus (just previously, in verse 4). But this makes Jesus' words rather superfluous – a man must be born physically before he can be born spiritually! By definition, 'a man' has already been born and before birth is not 'a man'. This view seems like a rather feeble attempt to make 'water' irrelevant to the discussion, as having no significant part in the new birth.

(ii) Others take 'water' metaphorically, not literally. It is treated as a symbol, either of 'the Word' (anything from the spoken gospel to the written scripture) or of 'the Spirit'. Actually, the Bible does not use 'water' as a synonym for 'word' (Ephesians 5:26 is often quoted as such, but a careful reading shows otherwise; it is not 'the water of the word'). If it is a metaphor for 'Spirit', Jesus is again guilty of tautology (unnecessary repetition) – 'must be born of Spirit and Spirit'. Elsewhere in the Gospel the Spirit is described as 'water' but with a qualifying adjective (like 'living', for example). 'Water' by itself means 'water', as everywhere in these opening chapters (1:31,33; 2:7,9; 3:23; 4:7).

(iii) Catholics, and many Protestants, take 'water' as a reference to the sacrament of baptism, in which literal water has a spiritual purpose and result. Such 'sacramentalists' then run 'water and Spirit' together into the belief called 'baptismal regeneration'. The new birth is therefore identified with baptism, 'water and Spirit' combining in this single event. So a man was 'born again' when he was baptised, even if this happened when he was still a baby (the Anglican Prayer Book reflects this view in its liturgy for Infant Baptism and for Confirmation).

Must we choose between these different interpretations? Is there some truth in each of them? Could they be partly right and partly wrong? Have they each seen part of the truth but not the whole of it? It certainly requires a considerable degree of disciplined open-mindedness to make a fresh approach, free from the teaching we have received and the traditions in which we have been brought up. Let's look again at what Jesus said, seeking a fresh understanding that fits text and content.

The phrase 'out of water and Spirit' is clearly the key. The two are distinct from each other yet closely related, each playing a part in bringing about the birth. The preposition ('out of') points to an emergence from a state of being submerged in both. The language is appropriate for baptism in each case – not least because of the absence of definite articles.

So I believe it is right to see 'water' as a reference to water baptism. This fits well into a conversation with Nicodemus. Pharisees refused John's baptism. And his opening remark flattered Jesus but probably disparaged John (note the emphatic '*you* are from God . . . God is with *you*, because *you* do miracles'). Jesus always reacted strongly to any attempt to drive a wedge between himself and John (4:3), claiming that both had the same authority and mandate (Mark 11:27-33). On that occasion he spoke about 'John's baptism' to the chief priests, teachers of the law (of whom Nicodemus was one, 3:10) and the elders, all of whom had refused to be baptised. It is therefore understandable that Jesus would bring this up, not least because Nicodemus was unwilling to be seen with Jesus, never mind confessing his sins publicly before John.

But I cannot believe that baptism by itself can bring about the new birth, especially in the absence of repentance and faith, as is inevitably the case with babies. That would be nearer the magical than the miraculous, encouraging irrational superstition. However, even given a penitent believing recipient, water baptism is not enough.

The same preposition ('out of') governing both water and Spirit strongly suggests an analogy between the two. If 'water' means water baptism, it would be natural to take 'Spirit' to mean Spirit baptism. In his following remarks, Jesus omits the definite article consistently: 'Spirit gives birth to spirit . . . so it is with everyone born out of Spirit' (3:6-8). This fits the concept of 'Spirit' as the medium rather than the agent of the new birth and is in marked contrast to the way Jesus later spoke about '*the* Spirit' as a person (in chapters 14-16).

So sacramentalists are right to see water baptism as an integral element in the new birth, but wrong to think that this is the same thing as Spirit baptism. And evangelicals are right to identify Spirit baptism with the new birth, but wrong to separate this from the practice of water baptism and the preaching of Spirit baptism. The reason for this silence will become apparent later in this book; we can simply say here that it is largely a reluctance to accept the 'Lukan' description of Spirit baptism in Acts as a definite and discernible experience, whereas neither Paul nor John give it any specific content, leaving its definition wide open.

If the reader does not agree with my conclusion about

this passage, I trust this will not be used to dismiss the rest of my thesis. I could have omitted this section and the main thrust of this volume would not have been affected, for it does not rest on this. Honesty compelled me to include it, largely because of the sacramental and evangelical interpretations, neither of which I find satisfactory but both of which have tended to suppress the proclamation of Jesus as baptiser in holy Spirit.

At the end of this chapter, we are told that God gives (continuous present) 'the spirit' to Jesus 'without limit' (3:34). That is why he was able to exhibit *all* the gifts, graces and fruit of the Spirit in himself.

Chapter 4 The story of the woman at the well, the bad Samaritan, is too familiar to need retelling. Not all notice that Jesus never got the water he asked for; nor did she get the 'living water' she asked for! Neither was frustrated; both were satisfied in other ways.

Jesus' offer needs to be unpacked: 'Whoever drinks the water I will give him will never thirst' (4:14). The tenses of the two verbs are significant. 'Give' is future, because Jesus could not dispense 'living water' at the time he was speaking (see below on 7:39). 'Drinks' is aorist, in Greek a single action. Only one drink will be sufficient to satisfy all future need, because it will release within the drinker 'a spring of water welling up to eternal life'. The external source of refreshment will become an internal (and eternal) resource. This one-off drink is mentioned by Paul, where he is describing baptism in Spirit (1 Cor. 12:13).

Of course, this chapter does not identify 'living water' as the Spirit, but the next chapter we look at specifically makes this identification.

Chapter 7 On the 'last and greatest day of the Feast (of Tabernacles)', it was the custom of the high priest to go down the hill to the pool of Siloam, returning to the temple with a pitcher of water which he poured on the altar, accompanied by prayers for rain. After the annual dry season, about six months, the 'early rains' of autumn were urgently needed to prepare the ground for the next year's crops, as well as to refill the cisterns with drinking water.

It was in the middle of this ceremony that Jesus shouted an invitation to the gathered crowd. 'If anyone is thirsty, let him come to me and drink. Whoever believes in me, as the Scripture has said, streams of living water will flow from within him' (7:37-8). It is exactly the same offer as that made earlier to the Samaritan woman. It is a little difficult to know which Old Testament prophecies he was referring to (there have been many suggestions, of which Isaiah 58:11 is as good as any). What is in no doubt is that the spring yielding streams of living water is the indwelling Spirit, which John's explanation makes crystal clear (forgive the pun!): 'By this he meant the Spirit, whom those who believed in him were later to receive. Up to that time, (the) Spirit had not been (given), since Jesus had not yet been glorified' (7:39; the words in brackets are not in the original text and have been added by translators).

There is an unusual construction here, literally translated: 'not yet was Spirit'. The meaning is clear and in English really requires an additional word like 'available' or, more usually, 'given'. The same kind of thing is found in Acts, where 19:2 says: 'We have not even heard that holy Spirit is'; this does not mean that they had never heard of the Spirit, for they were disciples of John the baptiser, who was always teaching about the Spirit – but again, 'given' or 'available' needs to be supplied to bring out the sense.

Note that for the first disciples there was a considerable time-gap between believing in Jesus and receiving the Spirit. The important thing is not whether these happen far apart or close together in time, but that they are two quite different things, as will become clear in Acts.

The reason for this long delay is that the 'living water' of the Spirit could not be drunk until Jesus had been 'glorified'. This word is used of his crucifixion, resurrection and ascension and must not be limited to anything less than these three events held together. The Synoptics, this Gospel and Acts all agree that Jesus had to return to heaven before he could pour out the promised Spirit (Acts 2:33).

Finally, note that 'receive' is used, rather than 'baptised', yet it clearly refers to the same event. The two are synonymous.

Chapters 14-16 These chapters are taken together, as covering one discourse of Jesus, given to his eleven disciples on the last night before he died. Scattered through it are a number of references to the Spirit.

The striking feature is that now the Spirit is specifically spoken about as a person rather than a power, 'he' rather than 'it'. Not 'she', either. There is a modern effort to discover femininity in the Godhead, one example of which believes the Spirit is female. It is true that prior to this fuller revelation words of the feminine gender are used for the Spirit of God (as human attributes or organs can be, as well as divine; 'breast' is a feminine word in Revelation 1:13, but this does not mean that Jesus now has a female form, though some feminist theologians assert this).

However, the full and final revelation that the Spirit is a person uses only male gender terms. Indeed, the whole Bible consistently refers to all three persons of the Trinity as 'he' or 'him'. God is King, not queen; Father, not mother; Husband, not wife. His Spirit is to be thought of in the same gender (for more teaching on this, see my book: *Leadership is Male*). I only mention the matter here because of the increasing confusion about the Holy Spirit himself.

In keeping with his personhood, the definite article is now used: '*the* Spirit', almost a name. Titles are used: 'the Spirit of truth' and, particularly, 'the Comforter'. This latter is rather too soft in English (sounding like a hot-water bottle or a security blanket!), though it rightly has 'fort' in the middle. 'Defender' or 'Counsellor' would be better, but both are probably too limited in application. The Greek word is *parakletos*, made up of 'beside' and 'call', someone called to stand by one in a crisis. A comforting prospect indeed!

Jesus calls him 'another' standby. There are two Greek words that could have been used here; one means 'another unlike this one', the other means 'another just like this one'. It is the latter here. The Spirit will be just like Jesus. The support and encouragement will be the same. He also will teach, explaining the things they have already heard and bringing new understanding until he has led them into 'all truth' (16:13). He will 'convict the world of guilt in regard to sin and righteousness and judgment' (16:8).

But all this tells us what he will do after he has come. Our immediate concern is with the beginning of his work. Do these chapters have anything to say about that?

One statement is particularly relevant: 'The world cannot receive him, because it neither sees him nor knows him' (14:17a). The Spirit simply cannot be given to unbelievers. They have neither the perception nor the experience to enable them to become intimately related to him. There must be some understanding before there can be an encounter. This categorical assertion of Jesus is a healthy antidote to current notions that the Holy Spirit is more likely to be found in the world than in the Church. There is a tiny truth in this. Many churchgoers have no experience of the Spirit and those who have will experience more of him by going into the world rather than by staying in church. But it remains true that the Spirit does not inhabit unbelievers.

The verse continues: 'But you know him, for he lives with you and will be in you' (14:17b). Some scholars have difficulty with the prepositions, implying as they do a quite radical change in the relationship. Some later manuscripts change the second part to 'and is in you', so that both halves mean the same thing: 'he is with you and in you'. But on the established textual principle that the more difficult version is to be preferred (because it is much more likely to have been made easier than harder to accept), I am staying with that. There is to be such a change for the disciples. From what to what?

Jesus is saying that they have already had some acquaintance with the Spirit, presumably both his presence and his power. He had already lived 'with' (i.e. alongside) them, in the person of Jesus himself, full of the Spirit. They had heard the messages and seen the miracles, all done in the Spirit. For three years, they had been eating, sleeping, walking and talking with the Spirit in their master. Is that all that is meant by 'with'? It is certainly enough. But Jesus had sent them out two by two, away from his presence, to duplicate his ministry in many places, demonstrating and then declaring the kingdom of God, healing diseases and casting out demons. Jesus could only do this by the power of the Spirit (Matt. 12:28). How could the disciples possibly have done the same unless the Spirit was 'with' them, even though they did not realise it? They were certainly conscious of supernatural power: 'Lord, even the demons submit to us in your name' (Luke 10:17; note that they attributed this to 'Jesus', whereas he attributed it to the Spirit).

So what was the future relationship to be? What Jesus seems to be saying is that the Spirit was still *outside*, even if alongside, them. But he would be *inside* them in the future. The unconscious relationship would become fully conscious. They would know him more fully, talk about him freely, relate to him as personally as they had to Jesus and look to him for support and guidance. None of this was already happening – but it would after he became their 'indwelling' Spirit.

There is little argument about when this change would take place. Pentecost is the obvious occasion, after which equal prominence is given to the name of Jesus and the Holy Spirit (about forty times each in the first few chapters of Acts). The Spirit was living 'in' them after they were 'baptised in holy Spirit'. That is when they 'received' him (see below, on 20:22).

One final comment on this verse is called for. The disciples were in a unique situation, having believed in Jesus before he had died, risen and ascended. They were therefore in a 'transitional' state, having to wait for what was later immediately available. This double phase in their relationship with the Spirit cannot be set as a precedent for later Christian experience, as if every believer has to pass through 'with' and 'in' stages. Nevertheless, as we shall discover in Acts, something like this could happen after Pentecost and could be the case right up to the present.

One other mention of the Spirit demands attention: 'He will not speak on his own; he will speak only what he hears, and he will tell you what is yet to come. He will bring glory to me by taking from what is mine and making it known to you' (16:13-14). Many have used this as a reason not to talk about the Holy Spirit. They seem to think he wants all the attention to be on Jesus, that he is somewhat shy and retiring, preferring to remain in the background. They are happy to speak about 'receiving' Jesus (which apostolic evangelism after Pentecost never did), but don't feel comfortable with exhorting others to 'receive the Spirit'. I have the feeling that these notions are more of an excuse, to cover up a lack of personal intimacy with the Spirit. Few enjoy talking about what they don't know. Actually, everything Jesus says about the Spirit here, he says about himself elsewhere: he only said what he heard from his Father, his delight was to bring glory to the Father. So on the basis of this reasoning, we shouldn't give any attention or prominence to Jesus either, but give it all to God! That is manifestly absurd in the light of the New Testament.

Chapter 20 We have reached one of the two most critical verses in building a doctrine of Spirit baptism (20:22; the other is 1 Cor. 12:13). It is no exaggeration to say that the interpretation of both texts has the most far-reaching effects on preaching and practising the gospel, to this very day. The divide between 'pentecostals' and 'evangelicals' will continue until a common understanding of them has been reached.

It is the evening of the first 'Easter' Sunday. The risen Jesus is meeting his disciples in the upper room, probably where the last supper was eaten a few days before. Already Jesus is commissioning them for a mission to the world: 'As the Father has sent me, I am sending you' (20:21; the verb 'send' in Greek is *apostello*; an 'apostle' is simply someone who has been sent by someone else to somewhere else to do something else). As in Luke's account, this mission centres on forgiveness, though here there is the added authority to retain as well as to remit sins, presumably where there is no real repentance.

In the middle of all this, Jesus says and does something unique: 'And with that he breathed on them and said, "Receive holy Spirit"' (20:22; the definite article is missing again).

Why is this single verse so crucial – and so controversial? Because without it everything would be much more straightforward. All the previous promises of receiving the Spirit would then relate to the day of Pentecost. But here is an event seven weeks earlier which appears to fulfil those promises, at least for some. Much more is at stake than the clarification of the sequence of events.

Whole theologies of 'conversion' have been built on this single verse. It has been used to deny that 'receiving' and 'baptised in' are simultaneous and synonymous – on the grounds that the disciples 'received' seven weeks before they were 'baptised'. It has been used to teach that every Christian needs to receive the Spirit *twice*, once for 'salvation' and subsequently for 'service', on the grounds that the disciples 'received' the Spirit on Easter Sunday evening and again on Pentecost Sunday morning.

Some pentecostal teachers go even further. Not only was this the reception of the Spirit, they say, it was also the regeneration of the disciples, the moment when they were 'born again', supporting the notion that baptism in Spirit is a 'second blessing' for those who have already been regenerated some time before (the technical name for this is 'subsequence', one of their two distinct doctrines; the other is 'evidence', that the only acceptable proof is speaking in tongues).

At the opposite extreme, liberal scholars tend to call this 'the Johannine Pentecost', claiming John has moved the date of that event back a few weeks so that he can include it in his Gospel. It is 'poetic licence' to include it in the day of resurrection, but it is John's way of linking the outpouring of the Spirit to the risen Lord. But this is to accuse John of historical inaccuracy, even deliberate dishonesty, in order to prove a point. That is not an acceptable solution to the apparent contradiction.

The dilemma may be boiled down to a simple question: did the disciples 'receive holy Spirit' on Easter Sunday or did they not? There are many reasons for doubting that they did, including the following:

(i) There is no statement that they did. It is an inference which may or may not be valid. Nothing is said about the disciples at all and no 'effects' are recorded. Nor did they do anything as a result.

(ii) Only ten were present. Thomas was missing. When did he receive the Spirit? And what about the rest of the 120 who were 'baptised in the Spirit' at Pentecost? When did they 'receive'?

(iii) When Peter later referred back to their receiving the Spirit, he dated it at Pentecost, not Easter Sunday.

(iv) Jesus blew on them *before* telling them to receive (actually, the best text omits 'on them' and simply says: 'he blew', though the unusual verb is actually 'he inflated'). Had his action 'breathed' the Spirit into them (as God breathed into the dust to make Adam a 'living soul' in Genesis 2:7), it would have been quite unnecessary to add the command: 'Receive'. He should have said something like: 'Now you have received...' The indicative mood would have been more appropriate than the imperative. Nor did they take any steps to obey this command. How did Jesus expect them to?

(v) The Spirit could not have been given yet, because Jesus had not been fully 'glorified'. He had not yet ascended, returned to his Father in heaven. He had made it clear that the Spirit could not come until he went (16:7).

(vi) There is no record of such a 'reception' of the Spirit on Easter Sunday anywhere else in the New Testament. If they really did 'receive' then, this was a very important event in their experience, whether we go on to say this is when they were born again, regenerated, or not (though that would make it even more significant). The other three Gospels ignore it. And this would be the only verse in all four Gospels that did not look beyond the time covered by their records for such a 'reception'.

(vii) Peter specifically states, in his sermon at Pentecost, that Jesus did not receive the promised Spirit to pour out on others until he was 'exalted to the right hand of God' (Acts 2:33).

We could add others, but that's enough to be going on with!

What, then, are we left with? No more and no less than what is explicitly stated. On that first day of the week, the risen Jesus gave them a sign and a command. That's all. Anything else is *eis*egesis (reading into the text what is not there), not *ex*egesis (reading out of the text what is there).

The sign and the command are then seen as a preparation for Pentecost some weeks later, a rehearsal of that all-important event. How would they know when to 'receive' the Spirit? They would hear Jesus blowing from heaven, the sound of a rushing mighty wind. Then they must 'receive' by surrendering to whatever the Spirit led them to do or say.

Jesus' 'proleptic' action (acting out the future) took place in the same location as a previous one, when he broke bread before his body was broken and gave wine to drink before his blood was shed. Jesus was a superb teacher, constantly preparing his disciples for what lay ahead. His deed and word on that Sunday were all of a piece with his foresight and method. And it made sure for ever that Pentecost would be directly linked to him and his ministry of baptising in holy Spirit.

To read anything more into John 20:22 is surely due to a theological prejudice seeking justification. But suppose my presentation has not convinced you. I would simply point out that other interpretations still fail to prove two things, often stated dogmatically as valid inferences.

First, even if these disciples did 'receive' the Spirit

on this occasion, that certainly does not prove that this was also their 'regeneration', the day they were 'born again'. They had already believed in the name of Jesus (in 1:12, that was enough to be 'born of God' during the transitional period before Pentecost; note that 'received' is past tense, referring to the time when Jesus came to his own Jewish people, some of whom 'received' him in the flesh while others rejected him). They were 'already clean', before Jesus died (13:10).

Second, even if these disciples did have two 'receptions' of the Spirit (which is far from established), there is no indication whatever that this would be a precedent for anyone else. Nowhere else in the New Testament is there a trace of this double experience. The later disciples received the Spirit once and once-for-all. They drank once and then enjoyed the streams of living water from the spring within them. They were neither exhorted to seek nor did they experience a 'second' crisis of blessing. Once they had received the Spirit, they only needed to walk in the Spirit, to go on being filled with the Spirit, exercising his gifts and producing his fruit. But we are jumping ahead again – into the Epistles. Before that we must look at Acts.

One final word about this crucial verse. No important doctrine should be based on just one verse, especially when it is built on what that verse doesn't actually say but on inferences drawn from it. That is altogether too flimsy a foundation for the construction erected on it.

ACTS – DURING

Without Acts we might discover *why* people need to be baptised in Spirit as well as *who* gives it and who receives it. But we would have little or no idea *how* or *when* it may be expected to happen. That is because the only description we have is in this one book of the New Testament.

Its author, Dr Luke, does not use the phraseology himself, but twice quotes it on the lips of others – Jesus and Peter (1:5; 11:16). However, both times the words are directly linked to events which he does describe. And both are, like the references in the Gospels, future tense, looking forward. But Jesus uses the phrase only 'a few days' before it happened for the first time and Peter, quoting his exact words, is actually applying them to something that has already happened. So Acts looks forward and back, but the bulk of the book looks mainly *at* what was occurring in the present. It is, as someone has aptly said, 'written on location'. It is, directly or indirectly, an eye-witness account of what happened in the earliest decades of church life, including baptisms in water and in holy Spirit.

The good doctor went out of the way to be as accurate as possible, to present a reliable record based on careful research (see the preface to his first volume, Luke 1:1-4). He was probably writing a brief for the judge or defence counsel ('most excellent Theophilus') at Paul's trial for his life in Rome. This would account for many features, including his full report of Jesus' and Paul's previous trials in which both were declared innocent three times, and the surprisingly extended account of Paul's final shipwreck (there were others), when he saved the lives of everyone on board, including his guards, with no thought of escaping himself.

This preamble of mine is intended to silence critics of Acts who support their position by questioning Luke's integrity, even suggesting that he has 'coloured' his narrative with his own preference, even prejudice, overemphasising the 'sensational' and 'abnormal' work of the Spirit. They usually fail to substantiate his motive. What purpose could such exaggeration achieve, especially under cross-examination in a court of law? And doctors are not usually purveyors of hyperbole, nor are they given to gullibility!

Earlier we noted that those who wish to give their own definition to Spirit baptism tend to dismiss Acts from consideration, usually on one of two grounds. One is that 'Acts is not didactic' – it is intended as 'narrative' only, of considerable interest but not to be used for instruction. The other is that 'Luke was not a theologian', not a recognised teacher in the church. Neither objection can stand up to examination (see our earlier critique). Neither prevents us from finding truth, spiritual as well as historical, within these pages.

However, it is true that there were both 'normal' and 'abnormal' features in the recorded cases of Spirit baptism and these must be carefully distinguished. For example, it would be naïve to claim that only those who have heard the sound of a rushing mighty wind have been genuinely baptised in holy Spirit (while I do know of this happening, I've never met anyone who insisted it was an essential evidence). Which brings us to the very first occasion.

Pentecost One of the final instructions Jesus gave before he returned to heaven was that his disciples should wait in Jersusalem until they were 'clothed with power from on high' (Luke 24:49; Acts 1:4). This would happen very shortly after his departure: 'For John baptised in water, but in a few days you will be baptised in holy Spirit' (Acts 1:5). Note how close this wording is to John's. The main change is in the second verb, from active to passive, from 'he will baptise you' to 'you will be baptised'. Why didn't Jesus say, 'I will baptise you'? Perhaps he wanted to focus their expectancy on what would be done for them, rather than on who would be doing it, which in any case they already knew.

Jesus went on to emphasise that when this all happened they would receive *power*, a shift in focus from John's concern for *purity*, but it would be wrong to make either exclusive of the other. It is only a change of emphasis, relative to the context of becoming 'witnesses . . . to the ends of the earth' (1:8).

'In a few days' must also have told them when it would happen, since that would be one of the three great annual feasts, Pentecost, when Jews thanked God for giving the law at Sinai, just fifty days after the 'passover' lamb had been sacrificed in Egypt. How appropriate, therefore, that the Spirit would be given at this feast, not to replace the law but to write it on their hearts. There is another intriguing link – when the law was given, three thousand were destroyed (Exod. 32:28); when the Spirit is given, the same number are saved (Acts 2:41). As Paul would later write: 'the letter kills, but the Spirit gives life' (2 Cor. 3:6).

Where did it happen? Almost certainly in the temple, in Solomon's porch, now the location of the El Aqsa mosque. It had to be a place that would hold thousands, since the crowd came to the disciples; the only move among them was that twelve of the one hundred and twenty stood up. Nine o' clock in the morning was the hour of public prayer.

What happened? A sound 'like' wind whistled round their heads inside the huge building. Jesus was blowing on them again, this time from heaven (by coincidence, there is a howling gale around the garden shed in which I am writing this). Flames 'like' fire settled on each head (were they burning down rather than up, the tips touching their heads or did separate flames burn up from each head? We don't know, but bishops' mitres are said to represent the latter). These phenomena were heard and seen by the disciples united in prayer (with open eyes, as was the biblical way). But the general public were not, apparently, aware of either. Nor were they repeated on any other occasions. It seems right, therefore, to think of them as abnormal, supernatural signs pointing to a unique occasion, the very first Spirit baptism.

These external objective entities led to an internal subjective experience: 'All of them were filled with holy Spirit and began to speak in other languages as the Spirit enabled them' (2:4; why do translators use the word 'tongues', which immediately suggests meaningless babbling? The Greek word, *glossolalia*, refers to proper speech with syntax and grammar). This single verse describes what happened to them, as distinct from what had previously happened around them.

We note first that 'filled with' is a synonym for 'baptised in' (cf. 1:5 with 2:4), though it is the only synonym that apparently can be used for later experiences of the Spirit by the same people (e.g. 4:31 and Eph. 5:18). All the other synonyms are used only of the first initiation.

The Spirit came from outside but got right inside. They were filled up, to the conscious exclusion of all else. They were filled to overflowing! How did this overflow manifest itself?

It is highly significant that no *emotional* state is mentioned, neither strong feelings of excitement and exuberance nor the quieter ones like joy or peace. In fact, the only emotions mentioned are those of the gathering crowd – amazement and disgust.

Nor is there any recorded *physical* reaction, like falling on the floor (they were already sitting on it), shaking or leaping up and down. Even if this did happen (though there is no indication whatever that it did), this was not why sceptics accused them of being drunk (it was the noise they were making and the fact that all were talking and no one was listening!).

The only recorded result of their being filled with holy Spirit is *verbal* – inspired speech, which some scholars refer to as 'prophetic charisms'. They were filled to overflowing and the overflow came out of their mouths. What came out was clearly supernatural. Unsophisticated Galileans from 'up north' were fluent in a variety of languages they could not possibly have picked up in their primary education.

In passing, it is worth pointing out that this was a co-operative activity. It was 'they' who began to speak, not the Holy Spirit. His part was to 'give them utterance'. That is, he told them what to say, by manipulating their tongues and lips to produce the right sounds, but they were responsible for activating the voice-boxes in their throats. Those who have never 'spoken in tongues' may find this a little difficult to comprehend but the fact remains that until someone begins to speak, no words will ever come (those who wait silently with open mouths expecting the Spirit to start speaking will be disappointed). All supernatural gifts are the same. The Spirit supplies the ability, but not the action. That is our responsibility and is always as much an act of faith as when Peter stepped out of the boat after Jesus told him he, too, could walk on the water; he only found he could when he did, though his faith quickly failed when he turned his attention from Jesus to the situation.

Peter regarded this phenomenon as coming within the general category of 'prophesying' and saw it as a fulfilment of Joel's prediction, which he quoted. Now all of them, like King Saul, were 'among the prophets'. Pentecost, if it means anything, inaugurates the prophethood of all believers! This aspect of the great event would be repeated, even if the wind and fire were not.

We are not told whether it was repeated in the three thousand baptised in water later the same day, but the language used by Peter makes it possible and even highly probable. In his preaching he had said: 'Exalted to the right hand of God, he [Jesus] has received from the Father the *promised* Holy Spirit [literally, 'the promise the Spirit the holy', a trinity of definite articles!] and has poured out what you now *see and hear*' (2:33; italics mine). When his hearers demonstrated a change of heart, he counselled them to: 'Repent and be baptised, every one of you, in the name of Jesus Christ so that your sins may be forgiven. And *you* will receive the gift of the Holy Spirit. The *promise* is for *you* and your children [Greek *teknon*, descendant, as opposed to *teknion*, which means little child, baby, infant] and for all who are far off – for all whom the Lord our God will call' (2:38-9).

We begin our comments on these vital verses by noting that the 'promise' and 'gift' refer to the Spirit, not salvation or forgiveness, much less the new covenant, as many claim. And they apply to baptism in Spirit, not baptism in water. Above all, the promise is unlimited in time (descendants) and space (far off). It is limited only by God's call and a responding call (2:21, 39).

Now for the likely inference. Peter has told the crowd that what they have seen and heard in him and his companions is the fulfilment of a 'promise' for which *they* are also eligible – if they will repent and be baptised. It would have been impossible for them not to assume that what they have already seen in others will also be their experience. Imagine their reaction if all they got through baptism was wet! They would have been very disappointed, if not disillusioned. Suppose Peter had taken the line of many modern preachers and explained thus: 'What you saw and heard was very special just for us; you must accept the Spirit in faith, believing you have received, even though nothing happened.' It could have caused a riot! 'You said we could have what you've got; you've conned us.' A case for the Trades Descriptions Act? The idea that they received the same gift and promise without anything like the same result borders on the ridiculous. They could only have departed with doubts rather than assurance (remember, they didn't even have any New Testament scriptures on which to rest their confidence).

Actually, we don't need to imagine or speculate like this, though it helps to expose the unreality of some contemporary teaching. There is a much clearer indication later in Acts that these three thousand *did* have a 'pentecostal' experience (see below).

Before leaving this crucial passage and the events described in it, we must note that already a number of other synonyms are used for 'baptised in' Spirit. We have previously mentioned 'filled'. In this same context we find other verbs: 'poured out' (2:33) and 'come upon' (1:8, literally 'fall on', clearly referring to chapter 2). Later reports of the same event use 'received' (10:47) and 'given' (15:8). From now on we shall refer to all these, including some others found elsewhere, as 'pentecostal terminology'. We also include the nouns 'gift' and 'promise'. This helps in recognising many references to baptism in Spirit which do not use the term, particularly in the Epistles.

There have been many claims that the whole of this 'day of Pentecost' was unique, a historical event never to be repeated. It can be celebrated annually as the birthday of the Church, but we must not expect to experience what they experienced, or even part of it. It may have been a spectacular display at 'lift-off', but once in orbit the Church can run her course without such fireworks. Advocates of this scenario must, of course, deny that even the three thousand baptised on the same day shared anything of the initial experience. But they have to explain away, or at least explain, why Acts records at least three more similar happenings.

Post-Pentecost We shall consider each of these events separately and then look at them together. This dual approach can lead to some unexpected insights.

Chapter 8 The first post-Pentecost 'pentecost' resulted from the preaching of Philip, a 'deacon' full of Spirit (6:3), among the half-caste Samaritans in a city near the well where Jesus met the woman (John 4). They were now to drink that 'living water' he had promised her, but only after some difficulty and delay.

Philip had declared and demonstrated the gospel, both word and deed, in the power of the Spirit. They had responded wholeheartedly to what they had heard and seen. They repented of their sins, believed the good news about the kingdom of God and the name of Jesus Christ and were duly baptised in water. *But* they did *not* 'receive holy Spirit' (8:15-16). This raises a number of questions. Alas, most discussion focuses on the wrong ones!

A favourite debate, prompted by anxiety about our own condition, focuses on the issue of their state or status at this stage. Were they or were they not 'saved'? Could they or could they not be called 'Christians'? More simply, if they had died, would they have 'gone to heaven'? Later, I shall show that these are loaded questions which prejudice any discussion before it even begins. In particular, the word 'Christian' is a source of confusion, given the many definitions now current and its absence from any significant passage in the New Testament. Even 'saved' is misleading (see Chapter 7, where I expand on this). What we can say about these baptised believers is that their sins were forgiven (on the basis of Acts 2:38a). That would have ensured their destiny had they all perished in a sudden disaster. But the real issue is not what would have happened to them if they had immediately died but what would have happened to them had they gone on living, but without the holy Spirit. Those who enjoy discussing all this would do well to follow the example of the apostles, Peter and John. For them the situation was not a matter for debate, but for decisive action. The deficiency must be remedied as quickly as possible. It is a matter of life rather than death, a practical rather than a theological 'problem'.

Scholars and commentators, even the best of them, concentrate on a purely hypothetical issue: *why* was the Holy Spirit *not* given to them as baptised believers?

There is a clear consensus regarding the answer. God or Christ deliberately delayed the gift so that it would be received at the hands (literally) of representatives of the Jewish community in Jerusalem, thus maintaining the unity of the Church and avoiding the founding of two 'national denominations', one Jewish and one Samaritan. All very interesting, but pure speculation in spite of being quite a plausible theory. But there is not even a hint of this in scripture, on which it could be built. In any case, Philip was Jewish and had held a responsible post in Jerusalem. To point out that he was not an 'apostle', who had been 'scattered' rather than 'sent' from Jerusalem (8:4) seems rather irrelevant, since even Paul received the Spirit at the hands of an ordinary believer (Ananias; see 9:17). This point is usually made by those who believe 'confirmation' must be at the hands of a bishop in 'apostolic succession'.

By far the most important question, totally ignored by most, is: *how* did anyone *know* that the Samaritans had *not* received the Spirit? They had fulfilled the conditions, believed in God and Jesus and been baptised. There was even 'great joy in that city'. Most modern observers would have said: 'How can anyone possibly say they haven't?' But Philip, Peter and John *knew* they hadn't. How? There is only one possible answer. It is that, up till then, *every new believer had received the Spirit in an unmistakable manner comparable to the original event at Pentecost*. In the case of the Samaritans, it was the first occasion on which this had *not* happened. It was therefore 'abnormal', not because of what later happened but because of what had *not* already happened (10:45 is the exact reverse of this). In other words, a 'pentecostal' reception of the Spirit had been the continual and universal experience of all new believers since Pentecost, from the three thousand on. The Samaritans were the first exception to the rule.

The remedy was prayer. Jesus received the Spirit in response to prayer (Luke 3:21-2) and had encouraged persistent prayer for this 'gift' (Luke 11:13). The disciples had prayed before Pentecost (Acts 1:14). It was the obvious thing to do. However, in this case we have the first, but not the last, example of the 'laying on of hands' in prayer for the Spirit to 'come [fall] upon them' (8:16). Has this a human or a divine significance? Are the interceders simply identifying more closely with the one prayed for, intensifying their desire? Or do they expect to be used as the channel conveying the answer to their petition? We do not necessarily have to choose between them; it could be both. Other scriptures favour this, but perhaps emphasise the latter (e.g. Jesus himself laid hands on the sick for their healing). However, it must be pointed out that the hands are the channel, not the source, of the Spirit. It is not a case of the Spirit being passed on from one person who has received to another who hasn't. This would usurp Jesus' unique role as the baptiser in Spirit. The Spirit would not then be poured out by him from on high. The Spirit would be 'seeping through' rather than 'falling on'. There is no hint that Jesus has delegated this ability to dispense the Spirit to others, as if he had said: 'I've given you the Spirit; now you go and give the

Spirit to others.' He commanded us to baptise others in water but not in Spirit. I personally know of cases where someone has 'received' when under the hands of praying friends who have not (wasn't John's baptism effective, even though he had not been baptised?). It is important to remember that we receive the Spirit as a gift from Jesus. There are examples of others receiving the Spirit without having hands laid on (10:44 is the next event in Acts), though it does seem to have become a more general practice (19:6 and Heb. 6:2).

The exact wording of the results of the apostles' action indicates that the Samaritans received the Spirit one by one as the apostles moved around the gathering, rather than simultaneously as a group, in contrast to the day of Pentecost. But what happened as each 'received' must have been much the same, since it was obvious to any observer.

One observer, who '*saw* that the Spirit was given at the laying on of the apostles' hands' (8:18) was Simon the sorcerer, an impenitent baptised believer who wrongly assumed that Peter and John were just channels of the 'gift'. As a professional magician he had a reputation to keep up and offered to buy the trade secret of dispensing such an experience. This would put him on the giving side with the apostles, rather than the receiving end. He must have been shaken by Peter's sharp rebuke: 'To hell with you and your money!' (8:20; a loose paraphrase!). Without real repentance, even belief in Jesus and baptism in water cannot bring forgiveness (8:22), an important reminder for all evangelists and their converts. We may also assume that Simon would not have received the Spirit had the apostles got round to him before he blurted out his demand.

If there is one conclusion that must be drawn from this whole episode, it is that believing in Jesus and receiving the Spirit are different things, whether they are closely associated or widely separated in time. This distinction is disguised when enquirers are exhorted to 'receive Jesus', an invitation never used by the apostles after the heavens had 'received' him at his ascension. Their appeal was to repent towards God in heaven, to believe in Jesus at his right hand and to receive the Spirit sent to take his place on earth. More on that later!

Before leaving this chapter, there are one or two points of interest for us in variant manuscript readings in the story of the Ethiopian eunuch (8:26-40). One text records that Philip insisted on his profession of faith, that he believed with all his heart that 'Jesus Christ was the Son of God' (8:37; this verse is usually a footnote), before he would baptise him. Another copy (the so-called 'Western text') has a different version of verse 39: 'The Holy Spirit fell upon the eunuch, and an angel of the Lord snatched away Philip.' This later addition may stem from the event itself, but even if it doesn't it reflects an expectation that baptism in Spirit normally follows baptism in water. But there can be an exception to this.

Chapter 9 Few would question that Paul repented of his sin and believed in Jesus on the road to Damascus, somewhere on what are now called the Golan Heights, at the foot of Mount Hermon where Peter, James and John had had a dazzling glimpse of the Lord's glory. Yet they had not been blinded. They had seen a 'transfigured' Christ, but Paul was confronted by the ascended Christ, whose prayer had now been fully answered: 'And now, Father, glorify me in your presence with the glory I had with you before the world began' (John 17:5).

Yet Paul had to wait another three days before he could be baptised in water and in Spirit at the hands of Ananias, who was no more than 'a disciple' (9:10-19). At the same time, his blindness was cured.

Few details of his baptism in Spirit are given. The wording is actually: 'filled of Spirit holy', but we have already seen the verb 'filled' used as a synonym for 'baptised' (1:5 and 2:4). There is no mention of any resulting manifestation, though some draw an inference from Paul's later claim that he 'spoke in tongues' (in private, not publicly) more than all the Corinthians put together (1 Cor. 14:18; 'all' means more than 'any' of them). He also later said he had been 'baptised in one Spirit' as they had been (1 Cor. 12:13; see the next section).

Luke does not mention every aspect of 'conversion' every time. Such repetition would be tedious. Sometimes he omits repentance, sometimes faith, sometimes water baptism and sometimes reception of the Spirit. We should not read anything too significant into these omissions. He is simply highlighting those aspects which made the occasion meaningful (like the huge number of baptisms at Pentecost). A full picture of his understanding of the beginning of discipleship must be built up by putting all his accounts together. All four dimensions listed above appear in his account of Paul's evangelistic methods (19:1-7; see below).

Chapter 10 Cornelius was a Roman centurion, the second Gentile to receive the Spirit if the Ethiopian was the first. Both were 'God-fearers', who believed in and worshipped the God of Israel, while not having 'converted' to become a circumcised proselyte. Cornelius was already known for his prayers to God and gifts to the poor, a 'devout man' who was brought in touch with the apostle Peter by an angelic visitation. Through Peter, he was enlightened with the gospel of Jesus of Nazareth, whom 'God anointed with Holy Spirit and power' (10:38).

Peter's Jewish prejudice against accepting Gentile hospitality had been cured by a vision during his siesta on a Joppa rooftop. He had come to Caesarea with a number of 'circumcised believers' from that port. He was 'still preaching' to Cornelius and his household when 'the Holy Spirit came [fell] on all who heard the message' (10:44). This happened spontaneously (no hands were laid on them) and simultaneously (everyone at once, like Pentecost).

How was Peter aware of this astonishing interruption? How did he recognise that 'they have received the Holy Spirit'? Again, there is no mention of any emotional reactions or physical actions. The sole evidence recorded, as at Pentecost, is verbal. They were 'heard' to be 'speaking in tongues [other languages] and praising God' (10:46). Did they all do both? Or were they one and the same thing? Probably the answer to both is negative. There is no mention of the languages being recognised, so it would not be known whether these were praise or prayer or something else. Had it been praise, it would probably be recorded as: 'they praised God in tongues'. They certainly could not speak in another language and praise God in their own at the same time. The simplest explanation is that some spoke in tongues while others burst into praise.

The primary surprise was that Gentiles were having their own Pentecost. Peter had said that the promised gift of the Spirit was 'for all who are far off' (2:39). He had obviously failed to realise the full significance and application of his own words (not the only person to do so when preaching in the power of the Spirit). He had probably been thinking of Jews already dispersed around the then known world (the 'Diaspora'). Now his words rebounded on him with new force.

There was also a secondary surprise. They had not been baptised! Yet here they were, receiving the Spirit beforehand. Nor does the narrative mention their repentance or faith, though these are mentioned later (11:18; 15:9). It is the first, and the last, time that such a sequence is recorded in Acts. It struck Peter as so abnormal that his first thought was how soon they could be immersed in water, thus normalising the situation! Clearly he did not think baptism in Spirit superseded baptism in water or made it unnecessary (as some do today). Peter did not do the actual baptising, however, but left it to his friends from Joppa. Perhaps he wanted them to remember the baptism rather than the baptiser (which may have been the motive for Jesus and Paul, who also refrained; John 4:2; 1 Cor. 1:14).

The question arises as to why the Lord 'poured out' (note this 'pentecostal' synonym in verse 45 of chapter 10) his Spirit on them so quickly, in sharp contrast to the delay in the Samaritan situation. Again, the answer is speculative, but it is more likely that Peter would never have baptised them had he not been sure that they were eligible. He had already overcome his Jewish inhibitions to address them, and that is probably as far as he would have been prepared to go had God not intervened in this way.

Their reception of the Spirit was the one absolute proof that would convince Peter that God had, indeed, accepted them and that Peter must also accept them. This was the very argument that he used on three separate occasions to justify his pioneering action. The wording of his justification is highly significant.

First, to the brothers from Joppa, he said: 'They have received the Holy Spirit *just as we have*' (10:47). There is no reason for thinking that these Joppans had been among the 120 on the day of Pentecost. They were probably later converts. Yet they had already had the same experience as these Romans.

Second, to a group of 'circumcised believers' in Jerusalem, he made the same point twice: 'As I began to speak [10:34-43 was only the introduction to his sermon!], the Holy Spirit fell on them *as he had fallen on us* in beginning [this last phrase is usually taken to refer to the day of Pentecost itself, but the absence of the definite article means that it could be general rather than a specific reference: 'when we began'] . . . So if God gave them *the same gift as he gave us*, who believed in the Lord Jesus Christ, who was I to think that I could oppose God?' (11:15, 17). In between these two defensive statements is another important one: 'Then I remembered what the Lord had said, "John baptised in water, but you will be baptised in holy Spirit"' (11:16; he is quoting the risen Christ's words, recorded in 1:5). Peter realised that the experience of Cornelius and his household was as much a fulfilment of that promise as his own. They had been 'baptised in holy Spirit', just as on the day of Pentecost.

Third, Peter repeated his Caesarean encounter to what has been called 'the Council of Jerusalem', where the apostles and elders, together with the whole church, met to discuss whether Gentiles had to become Jews (and be circumcised) to be true disciples of the Jewish Messiah, Jesus the Christ: 'God, who knows the heart, showed that he accepted them by giving the Holy Spirit to them, *just as he did to us*. He made no distinction between us and them' (15:8-9). Again, Peter makes a general connection with all his hearers; he does not limit it to 'some of us' or 'those of us who were there on the day of Pentecost'.

All this supports our previous conclusion that a 'pentecostal' reception of the Spirit was universal in the early Church. The only abnormalities were in the timing or sequence, not in the experience itself. Also confirmed is the interchangeability of 'baptised in' and 'received'.

One final comment – the word 'household' is not the same as 'family', but more comprehensive, including any others living in the same property, especially slaves. It would be used as an equivalent of English 'staff'. Cornelius' family may have been back in Rome during his 'overseas posting'; he may not even have been married. What is certain is that there were no babies or infants in his 'household' at the time of Peter's visit. All were old enough to understand the message (10:33) and respond to it. They all repented (11:18) and all believed (15:9). The Spirit fell on 'all who heard the message' (10:44) and they were all baptised. Such qualifications occur in other cases of whole 'households' (e.g. 16:32-4; the 'whole household' of the Philippian jailer heard the word, believed, were baptised and filled with joy).

Chapter 19 Not the least interesting aspect of the events in Ephesus is the link between Luke and Paul, who are so often set in opposition to each other. Here Luke is describing Paul's evangelistic approach, with no trace of reservation. They often travelled together (usually indicated by the use of 'we'), though not here.

It is a tragedy that the Bible books have been cut up into chapters, often putting asunder what God had joined together. This is the case with chapters 18 and 19. The 'disciples' whom Paul encountered (19:1) had obviously been instructed by Apollos (18:24-8). This Alexandrian knew 'the Scriptures' (i.e. the Old Testament) so well that he could prove that Jesus was the expected Messiah, the Christ. With enthusiasm and accuracy he passed on the facts about Jesus – presumably his life, death, burial, resurrection and possibly his ascension. But there were limits to his knowledge and experience. He seems not to have got beyond the objective facts to the subjective need to have a personal faith in Jesus and be baptised into his name (he did know about baptism, but as practised by John in the Jordan, relating only to repentance and forgiveness). He does not seem to have been baptised in the Spirit, though he would certainly have known about it from John. Fortunately, Priscilla and Aquila filled out his spiritual education in their own home and wisely sent him elsewhere to exercise his enlarged ministry (it unsettles any congregation when the pastor apparently 'changes' to novel and radical notions he has not previously taught).

This background explains why Paul was puzzled by the Ephesian 'disciples'. He began by assuming they were true believers. After all, they knew the name 'Jesus' and could talk about him with some knowledge, especially the Hebrew prophecies that pointed forward to him. It was an understandable misunderstanding!

But there was something missing. Or was it someone? We are not told what aroused Paul's suspicions that all was not well. Clearly it was the absence of what he expected to be present in disciples of Jesus. Equally clearly, the missing element(s) were linked in his mind to the Spirit, which explains his first question to them: 'Did you receive Holy Spirit when you believed?' (19:2; no definite article). Some translations say 'since you believed'. Pentecostals insist on 'since' to support their claim that the Spirit is received *subsequently*, after conversion. Evangelicals insist on 'when' to support their claim that the Spirit is received *simultaneously*, at conversion. Actually, the Greek (*pisteusantes*, literally 'having believed') can be taken either way, so neither view can be based on it!

The conclusion that can and must be drawn from the question itself is that, for Paul, believing in Jesus and receiving the Spirit are two very different things. And one can happen without the other (as had already happened in Samaria; 8:16). Paul is asking whether both things have happened, whether they happened together or separately. There is nothing automatic or inevitable when it comes to believers receiving. Both are necessary to the full Christian life.

Those whose theology prevents them from recognising that anyone could believe without receiving are quick to point out that Paul soon discovered that they had not yet adequately 'believed in Jesus'. This is perfectly true, but does not invalidate the distinction between believing and receiving or the possibility that one may be present without the other. When Paul asked the question he suspected that this was exactly their situation. Otherwise, his question was utter nonsense. He might as well have asked: 'Did you become a Christian when you became a Christian?' if believing and receiving are virtually one and the same. It takes audacity to accuse such a trained legal mind of thinking up such a stupid question.

The translation of their reply is somewhat misleading.

'No, we have not even heard that there is a Holy Spirit' (19:2; NIV). It is extremely unlikely that disciples of John the baptiser would be in such total ignorance. What they actually said was: 'We have not heard that Holy Spirit is.' Just as translators added 'given' to 'Holy Spirit was not' (in John 7:39) to make sense in English, it needs to be supplied here for the same reason. They are saying that they had not been told that John's prediction had begun to be fulfilled.

Paul's second question is intriguing. Since he now knows that they have not received Holy Spirit, his immediate thought is not their belief, but their baptism. Clearly, in his mind, there is a close connection between water and Spirit baptism. The 'normal' course of events is for the latter to follow hard on the former.

They have been baptised, but only according to John's principles and practice. It was a baptism of repentance for forgiveness, but not an act of faith in Jesus. Yet another insight into Paul's thinking emerges at this point. Those who have not submitted to full Christian baptism are not yet true believers! There is an obedience to the gospel, an obedience of faith, which Paul taught (e.g. 2 Thess. 1:8).

So Paul now led them into personal faith in Jesus, baptising them 'into the *name* of the Lord Jesus'. This was an identification with his death, burial and resurrection (Rom. 6:3-4).

Those who cling to the fusion of 'believing' and 'receiving' have the same problem with the last part of the narrative as they think they can avoid with the first part.

There is still a gap in time between them, though it is now much shorter. Paul would surely not have baptised them unless he had some indication that they now believed in the Jesus into whose name they were being baptised. Yet they would not receive the Spirit until *after* their baptism, in fact not until Paul had laid hands on them.

As in every other recorded case, the evidence was verbal, this time other languages and 'prophecies' in their own language, both in the form of spontaneous inspired speech. Since it is unlikely that anyone else was present to recognise the 'tongues', we must assume that 'prophesied' refers to separate utterances and we do not know whether some spoke in one way and others in another or whether all did both alternately. The former seems more likely.

This group of 'about twelve men in all' (19:7; could no one make an exact count?) formed the nucleus for the outstanding church at Ephesus. We know more about it than any other in the New Testament. They did lapse from their initial love (Rev. 2:4) but recovered (according to the Church Father Ignatius). The apostle John lived here into old age, writing his Gospel and letters here and Revelation while exiled to the offshore island of Patmos. He also took Mary, the mother of Jesus, to live and die at Ephesus.

Paul wrote one of his finest letters to the Ephesians, which we will look at in the next section. There is a significant statement there, which links to the account we have just examined: 'Having believed [*pisteusantes* again] you were marked in him with a seal, the promised [reminiscent of Acts 2] Holy Spirit' (Eph. 1:13). When Paul wrote this, his first dealings with that group of men must have come back to mind.

We have come to an end of our studies in Acts, but we cannot end them here. There is more to be said.

There is a widespread evangelical teaching that all these occasions recorded in Acts were abnormal, not to be taken in any way as a precedent for receiving the Spirit now. The definite and even dramatic experiences were unique to that initial period and must not be expected to be repeated today. They are of interest to us, but were never intended for our situation.

These teachers would clearly be happier if the verbal phenomena had been confined to the day of Pentecost. What do they make of the fact that they were repeated on at least three other occasions (Samaria, Caesarea and Ephesus)? Well, they have an ingenious explanation, claiming that these also were unique. The repetitions are regarded as abnormal 'mini-Pentecosts', marking a radical new change in the spread of the gospel, when it reaches a new ethnic category. Appealing to 'You shall be my witnesses in Jerusalem, and in all Judea and Samaria, and to the ends of the earth' (Acts 1:8), the theory is that a special 'Pentecost' would mark each of these widening circles. Thus, Acts 2 is the Jewish Pentecost, Acts 8 the Samaritan Pentecost and Acts 10 the Gentile Pentecost. Very neat, but perhaps a little too neat. How does the Acts 19 Pentecost fit in? Of course, it doesn't. This was not a new ethnic milestone, but a throwback to a former day. It is usually dismissed from the series of 'Pentecosts' because John's disciples would 'probably soon die out anyway'! Actually, they didn't and years later the apostle John included many 'put-downs' in his Gospel to counteract this (John the baptiser 'was not that light'; he 'did no miracles'; he said 'the bride belongs to the bridegroom' and 'he must increase, I must decrease').

But we have already pointed out the rocks on which this theory is wrecked. Both the Samaritan and the Caesarean situations imply, in different ways, that their experience was the same as that of all the early disciples, from Pentecost onwards. The 'abnormalities' were in the timing – in one case, long after believing, and in the other, before being baptised. True, Luke records these major moves, to Samaritans and Gentiles, as unique stages in the story he tells. But the unusual feature is not *what* they experience but *who* is having the experience. Their baptism in Spirit was exactly the 'same' as everybody else, which was Peter's threefold claim when defending his acceptance of Cornelius' hospitality and household.

This 'triple-Pentecost' theory, as I will call it, usually goes hand in hand with the belief that believing in Jesus and receiving the Holy Spirit are one and the same. Our study of these same passages has shown, I hope conclusively, that this is not the case.

It is hardly surprising that those who hold these rather forced interpretations are eager to rule out Acts as a source of doctrine (either because 'Acts is not didactic' or because 'Luke was not a theologian'). The real reason for these objections is an unwillingness to accept the description of baptism in holy Spirit as a definite experience with discernible evidence. They are only too aware of the practical problems of applying this as a norm or standard for today's Church. Quite simply, too many would fail the test. We will deal with these implications later (in Chapter 7).

Having effectively removed Acts from consideration it no longer affects the interpretation of statements in the Epistles, particularly those written by Paul and John, concerning reception of the Spirit. So teachers are able to insert their own definition, since the Epistles themselves do not give one.

But Acts and the Epistles cover the same period, the same places and the same persons. There are narrative and 'didactic' sections in both, even if the ratio is different. Above all, both John and Paul are seen in Acts laying hands on believers so that they may receive the Spirit! The letters they later wrote were to those they had already ministered to. It is quite arbitrary to claim that the Epistles reveal a different understanding of the Spirit from that of Acts, creating an artificial division which can be dangerously misleading.

In this book, we shall study the Epistles in the light of what we have learned from Acts, gaining a unified and consistent picture of 'the apostles' doctrine' (Acts 2:42).

THE EPISTLES – AFTER

All the references to receiving (being baptised in) the Spirit look back to what has already happened, since all the New Testament Epistles are addressed to those already fully initiated by apostles into Christian discipleship. They are 'called saints' (e.g. Romans 1:7; later translators with ecclesiastical canonisation in their background demurred over the application of this title to all believers, so expanded it into 'called *to be saints*'!). But they are already 'holy ones' in principle and potential, by virtue of having received the *holy* Spirit.

There is another significant feature of the references in the Epistles. There is not a single description of what 'baptism in Spirit' is like. 'Pentecostal terminology', which focuses on the subjective or experiential aspects, is largely, though not entirely, missing. The phrase itself occurs only once (1 Cor. 12:13). Instead, the synonym 'received' and its counterpart 'given' are widely used.

This, of course, plays right into the hands of those who have a vested interest in claiming that the events recorded in Acts were all abnormal, so our 'doctrine' of Spirit baptism must be based on the 'didactic' Epistles. They are then free to assert that it happens automatically and even unconsciously at the moment a person believes in Jesus (they usually say 'receives' Jesus, unlike the apostles).

But there is a very simple explanation as to why the Epistles don't describe the experience. They are written to those who've already had it! Why tell them what they already know perfectly well and from first hand? The apostles don't waste words.

There is an exact parallel with water baptism. Not a single verse in the Epistles ever links the verb 'baptise' with the noun 'water'. Some evangelicals, basing their beliefs on the Epistles alone, teach that 'baptised' is a synonym for 'believed'! They claim that all who believe, whether they have any contact with physical water or not, have been 'baptised into Christ' (Gal. 3:27), even 'into his death' (Rom. 6:3); they have had the 'one baptism' (Eph. 4:5). This shows how easily the New Testament can be misused when one part of it is isolated from another. Every part must be interpreted in the light of the whole.

To sum up, the Epistles take for granted that every reader has experienced baptism in water and Spirit. There is not a single exhortation to seek either. From Acts we know that if either or both were missing, *immediate* steps were taken to remedy the deficiency. Not so today. There are people professing to follow Christ and even accepted into church membership who cannot be assumed to have these. So it is not possible to interpret 'we' or 'us' in the Epistles as covering every 'Christian' in the contemporary Church. We must constantly keep this caveat in mind.

We shall concentrate on those texts covering the initial gift of the Spirit. If we included all those relevant to the 'why' of baptism in Spirit, we would have to cover *every* reference to the Spirit and this book would be ten times the size! So we shall concentrate on a limited number of passages.

Pauline We have already studied Paul's *practice* (in Acts 19). Now we look at his *teaching*. If we do not hold these together, we could be accusing him of inconsistency. He practised what he preached and preached what he practised.

Romans 5:5 'God has poured out his love into our hearts through [Greek *dia*] Holy Spirit given to us.' Both 'poured out' and 'given' belong to what we have called 'pentecostal terminology' and clearly refer to the initial experience.

Love is one flavour of the single fruit of the Spirit (Gal. 5:22). It is God's love for his peoples (both Christians and Jews, see Romans 11:28) and for the whole world (John 3:16).

Romans 8:9 'And if anyone does not have the Spirit of Christ, he does not belong to Christ.' Few texts have been so widely mistranslated, misquoted and misapplied, usually by being taken out of context, as is so often the case.

The common interpretation actually reverses Paul's intended challenge. His negative statement which would exclude some is taken as a positive one to include all! The sense usually given to it is: this proves that every 'Christian' *must* have the Spirit. The text is then used to cancel the claim made in this book that 'believing in Jesus' and 'receiving the Spirit' are two different things and that one can happen without the other.

We must examine the text itself and, even more, the

context, if we are to get to grips with Paul's meaning. But I fear that the traditional way of understanding it is so widely used and so deeply entrenched that few will be able, never mind willing, to unlearn it. Anyway, here goes.

Where shall we begin? Obviously, the text itself. But what is invariably quoted is only half a text, half a verse. Why is it never quoted as a whole, to include the previous phrase: 'if the Spirit of God dwells in you'? These two 'ifs' (the first much stronger than the second) point to a parallel repetition, characteristic of Hebrew thinking (and of their poetry, as in the Psalms). The two clauses, including 'Spirit of God' and 'Spirit of Christ', need to be considered together. But before we do so we need to get them properly translated.

The second part does not have 'Christ' twice. To translate it as 'he does not belong to Christ' is a liberty of the translator. One version goes even further: 'he is no Christian'! It is literally 'he is not one of him'. Who does this refer to? The subject of both clauses is the Spirit, whether 'of God' or 'of Christ', so 'of him' could refer to the Spirit. Be that as it may, the definite article is missing from both clauses, indicating an emphasis on the power rather than the person of 'Spirit'.

Significantly, the tense of both verbs is present. Paul is not thinking of their past conversion, but their present condition, their '*now* . . . in Christ Jesus' (8:1). Furthermore, the present tense is also known as the 'continuous' tense, because it indicates not just a present happening but one that has extended from the past and will extend into the future. It is most clearly translated into English as to *go on* doing something.

We are now in a position to translate the whole verse properly: 'But you are not in flesh but in Spirit, if Spirit of God truly goes on residing in you; but if anyone does not go on having Spirit of Christ, this one is not of him.' This changes the whole thrust of Paul's challenge. He is not focusing on the second person of the Trinity, but the third ('Spirit' is mentioned four times in a single sentence). He is not talking about whether a person is a Christian or not, but whether a Christian is living in the Spirit or not.

The whole Epistle is addressed to Christians anyway, but this is particularly true of chapter 8. He has long since left the subject of justification behind and is now well into the theme of sanctification. This chapter could well be entitled: 'Life in the Spirit'. But such living is neither automatic nor inevitable.

The immediate, as well as the wider, context of verse 9 bears this out. It is full of the little word 'if' (eight times in verses 9-17). Here (and even more fully in Galatians 5), Paul faces his 'saints' with an alternative and therefore a choice. They can either live according to flesh, which is hostile to God, refuses to submit to his law and leads to death; or they can live according to Spirit, which brings peace with God and life to mortal bodies. They can't live according to both. It is quite literally a matter of life or death.

It is right in the middle of all this that Paul makes the statement that we are considering. It seems almost absurd that, right out of the blue, he should interject an aside, 'Of course, all this is irrelevant if you're not a Christian at all', which is how most people interpret it.

He is pointing out that believers can't go on living 'in Spirit' if they go on living 'in flesh'. Sooner or later, they run the danger of discovering that Spirit of God is no longer 'dwelling' in them; they are no longer 'having' Spirit of Christ. And that means 'death'.

This interpretation, which I believe is truer to text and context, raises the obvious question as to whether it is possible to lose the Holy Spirit, once he has been given. That is a separate issue (fully dealt with in my book: *Once Saved, Always Saved? A study in perseverance and inheritance*, Hodder and Stoughton, 1996). Our answer will depend on our understanding of 'death' and 'if' in this passage.

Romans 8:15 'You did not yet again receive a slavish spirit that made you fearful, but an adopting Spirit, which made you cry out: "Abba, Daddy!"' The contrast between cringing slaves and clinging sons was commonly observed in ancient households. 'Abba' was the first and most intimate term a Hebrew boy learned to use in addressing his father. No pious Jew would dare to use such a term of familiarity with respect to God. Yet Jesus used it in prayer and encouraged his disciples to do the same.

Paul uses 'received' here because he is contrasting spiritual with social experience. A slave is not 'baptised' into his terror. Note that the result of receiving the Spirit of adoption is to 'cry out'. The Greek verb (*krazein*) means spontaneous verbal ejaculation, as when the disciples cried out in fear when they thought they saw a ghost (Matt. 14:26); it was Jesus walking on the water. Peter also cried out when he accepted Jesus' invitation to do the same, but soon began to sink (Matt. 14:30). It is astonishing that this verse is so often described as 'the inward witness' of the Spirit, a silent witness. 'Crying out (loud)' is the exact opposite!

And 'Abba' would be a 'tongue', a foreign language, for Gentile converts in Rome (or Galatia, where they experienced the same release; Gal. 4:6). Once again, inspired supernatural speech is the evidence of the Spirit received, though presumably they would go on using this form of address whenever they prayed 'in Spirit' (Eph. 6:18). This continued intimacy would be the basis for confidence, providing an ongoing assurance that they had indeed been adopted as sons in God's family (Rom. 8:16; note that the verb is in the present continuous tense: 'goes on testifying'). And sons will one day be heirs of their father's property; believers will one day share in their elder brother's glory if they are willing to share the suffering he first had to go through (8:17, the last 'if' in the chapter; even 'glory' is not automatic or inevitable).

1 Corinthians 6:11 'And that is what some of you were [idolaters, thieves, drunkards, etc., listed in v. 10]. But you were washed, you were sanctified, you were justified in the name of the Lord Jesus Christ and in the Spirit of our God' (NIV wrongly puts 'by' for 'in', a change which has more serious implications in 1 Cor. 12:13).

'You were washed' may well refer to water baptism, but the last phrase 'in the Spirit' hints at Spirit baptism. Since both normally happened close together, both could be in mind. Since for us the different components of Christian initiation are often far apart in time, it is difficult for us to think like the apostles, who thought of them together, as parts of a whole without confusing the parts with each other. Hence they can, on different occasions, depending on their immediate purpose, describe the beginning of the Christian life as when they repented or when they believed (in Jesus) or when they were baptised or when they received (the Spirit) or, as here, when they were washed, when they were sanctified (not made holy in themselves yet but made holy to God, separated from sin and for him), when they were justified. There is no chronological order here or 'justified' would have come first. This is what happened to them at the start, what changed them from sinners into 'saints' (1:2 should read 'called holy', not 'called to be holy', or, better still, 'called saints'). Considering what they had been it could only have happened in the name of *Jesus* and in the *Spirit* of *God*, a miraculous intervention by the whole Trinity.

1 Corinthians 12:13 'For indeed we were all baptised in one Spirit into one body – whether Jews or Greeks, slave or free – and we were all given a drink of one Spirit.' Sad to say, this is not only the most crucial but by far the most controversial verse in all the Epistles.

That is because it is the *only* verse in the Epistles to use the phrase 'baptised in . . . Spirit' and too many have a vested interest in trying to prove it doesn't even occur here! Both pentecostals and evangelicals are embarrassed by its presence in this context.

But the Greek wording is *exactly* the same as the four references in the Gospels and the two in Acts – the same verb (*baptizein*), with the same preposition (*en*) and the same dative case for Spirit (*pneumati*). Before explaining how and why so many deny that it is the same phrase, we need to look at the rest of the statement.

It is a double statement, again reflecting Jewish 'parallelism' as a natural way of thinking and speaking for someone like Paul. We need to ask what each half means and how they relate to each other. Both verbs ('baptise' and 'drink') are passive; not so much something that they did so much as something that was done to them or for them. Even more important, both are in the aorist tense, referring to a single unrepeated event.

The critical question is whether the wording covers two events or two aspects of the same event. Both are 'liquid' verbs and both are clearly metaphorical, referring to the Spirit, that 'living water'. The only difference is that in one case the liquid was external (they have been 'immersed' in what was outside) and in the other it was internal (they have imbibed it so that it was inside).

This combination is identical with the day of Pentecost itself. They were 'baptised in' and 'filled with' Spirit in the one experience. It therefore seems more than reasonable to take the Corinthian duality in the same way. It was a complete saturation, inside and out. They were soaked and slaked at the same time!

However, there are some noticeable variations from previous usage, two in particular.

The first is a substitution. Instead of the usual 'holy', Paul has 'one', in both parts. He is certainly not using this as a proper name, but as a descriptive adjective. Just as John the baptiser had used 'in holy Spirit' to emphasise the *purity* this baptism should bring, Paul uses another aspect, 'in one Spirit', to emphasise the *unity* this baptism should bring.

The whole context in his letter and, indeed, the state of the church to which it is addressed, fully explain this variation. The exercise of 'spiritual gifts', none of which they lacked (1 Cor. 1:7), was not building up (edifying) but breaking up the church at Corinth. In the absence of love, fruit of the Spirit, gifts become dangerously divisive, especially when the more sensational (impressive sights or sounds) are more valued than the less spectacular. Paul teaches that all are equally necessary and that those they are tempted to despise are worthy of greater honour.

The theme of the whole of chapter 12 is 'variety in unity'. This applies to God himself. Father, Son and Spirit are different from each other, yet in perfect harmony. Their shared work in the Church is the same – a variety of gifts, service and working is the result. The Church is just like any human body – many different limbs and organs with different functions, yet making one whole organism through which the human spirit can operate in this world.

'So it is with Christ.' His Spirit needs a 'body' so that he can continue his mission in word and deed (Acts 1:1). The Church is that 'body', both locally and universally. There is only 'one Spirit' in this 'body', as in any other. Therefore the body must be united, not divided.

Paul appeals to the Corinthians by the memory of their introduction to this body. Their initiatory experiences were all of one and the same Spirit. They were therefore united from the very beginning and shared a single source for all their different gifts. They must now 'make every effort to keep the unity of the Spirit through the bond of peace' (Eph. 4:3), matching the exercise of 'gifts' with expression of 'fruit', particularly love (chapter 13 of 1 Corinthians picks this up, with its famous description of essential, effectual and eternal love; but the real climax to Paul's appeal is in chapter 14, in which he illustrates how the gifts, particularly tongues and prophecy, can be exercised in love, for the edification of the whole assembly).

The second variation is the addition of 'into one body' to 'baptised in one Spirit'. Both the reason why this extra phrase is included and its meaning are not in any dispute. It is the theme of the rest of the chapter and is another of the three times the word 'one' appears in this single verse. Could Paul make his point any clearer?

But the conjunction of two prepositions ('in' and 'into'), governed by the same verb ('baptised') calls for some attention. There is a parallel and a precedent in John's description of his activity in the Jordan: 'I baptise you *in* water *into* repentance' (Matt. 3:11). 'In' describes the medium in which the person is immersed and 'into' defines the reason or purpose of the immersion. So the objective of Spirit baptism is to integrate an individual into the body of Christ, to make them a member of the Church.

Membership of the Church today is more like the membership of a club – apply to join, have your name accepted, pay your subscription, take part in the programme of activities, attend and vote at the business meetings, etc. Nothing could be further from the New Testament concept. Members of a body are functional, each playing a vital service to the whole. A role, not a roll. If any part is lost, the whole body is 'dismembered'. If one suffers, all suffer (who says, 'My tooth has an ache'? Rather, 'I have a toothache'). If one rejoices, all rejoice. If one receives a spiritual gift, all have received it.

Baptism in Spirit creates this body because it releases the gifts in individuals, enabling them to fulfil a function that benefits the rest of the body. These 'manifestations' or new abilities enable the Church to continue the work of Jesus on earth, provided they are co-ordinated in love.

So far, so good! Why would anyone disagree with any of this? Why has there been so much argument about this verse? Why do most English versions translate this verse with a different wording to the one we have been expounding? Why are both pentecostals and evangelicals unhappy with it as it stands?

Pentecostals don't like it because it places baptism in Spirit at the very beginning of the Christian life, when being brought 'into the body'. Therefore, it properly belongs to the initial and not a later stage. This contradicts their doctrine of 'subsequence', that Spirit baptism is subsequent to 'conversion', a 'second blessing' for believers already 'in the body' and not needing to be baptised 'into' it.

They appeal to the fact that many translations have changed 'in' to 'by', making the Spirit the agent rather than the medium. So this being 'baptised *by* the Spirit' is said to be something altogether different from baptism *in* Spirit. It is regarded as a synonym for 'conversion' or regeneration and not necessarily a conscious experience at all. It is ironical that pentecostals, with a vested interest in finding 'baptism in Spirit' wherever possible in scripture, should take this line; but they are obviously not above rejecting texts that don't fit into their theory, a weakness to which we are all prone.

Evangelicals, too, have welcomed the change to 'by', thus separating this verse from baptism *in* Spirit, as referred to in the Gospels and Acts. Anxious to include all believers in the 'we' of this verse, they welcome the opportunity to divorce it from the definite experiences associated elsewhere with the preposition 'in'. They can then reassure converts that they have been baptised *by* one Spirit *into* one body when they believed, whether they experienced any baptism *in* Spirit or not. Baptism in Spirit is abnormal or optional, baptism by Spirit is normal and essential.

Of course, both run into some very basic problems. The preposition (*en* usually meaning 'in') is exactly the same here as everywhere else. Had the Spirit been the agent rather than the medium, the definite article would have been included (it is more than awkward to say 'baptised by Spirit'). And this would be the *only* verse in the entire New Testament referring to the Spirit as a baptiser, a rather slender foundation on which to base such an unusual doctrine.

I have not mentioned the 'sacramental' view of this verse, which is even less convincing. 'Baptised in Spirit' refers to water baptism and 'drinking Spirit' refers to the other sacrament of communion! Augustine held this view, so many Catholics and Protestants (including Luther and Calvin) have followed him. As we have seen, 'drunk' is in the aorist tense, referring to a one-off non-repeated action and drinking Spirit has never been a metaphor for drinking the 'blood', much less eating the 'body'.

We shall say more about all these approaches when we look at the history of Spirit baptism (in Chapter 5). Meanwhile, let us summarise our findings.

Paul's overriding concern is for the unity of the body, which neutralises even racial and social divisions ('Jew and Greek, slave and free'). He appeals on the ground of their common initial experience of being immersed in and imbibing one Spirit, releasing them into functional membership within the one body of Christ. He speaks of this as an event of which they were fully conscious and can easily recall. He shares this experience with them ('we', not 'you'), though his was at a different time and place. This 'we' must be limited to himself and those he addresses. It cannot be applied to all 'Christians' today any more than if he had said, 'We were all baptised in water', which would also have been true for himself and the Corinthians. The New Testament contains no such person as an unbaptised 'saint', unlike the Church of today.

Above all, we have established that 'baptised in one Spirit' in this Epistle refers to exactly the same event and experience as 'baptised in holy Spirit' in the Gospels and Acts. The simple explanation for the change in adjectives is that, at the time they were speaking, John's primary concern was for the purity of God's people whereas Paul's was for their unity. Both used the same preposition: 'in'.

That is why I have given my book its rather wordy title: *Jesus Baptises in One Holy Spirit*. I wanted to combine all the New Testament statements in one. I wonder how many realised this when they first picked it up? Had anyone done so, they would have saved some money, because they could have deduced the direction and conclusion of my thinking! However, I trust they will feel they got their money's worth of new insights.

2 Corinthians 1:21-2 'Now the one who makes us with you firm in Christ, having anointed us, is God, having both sealed us and given us the deposit of the Spirit.'

The Spirit brings us stability, as well as purity and unity. Those who walk in the Spirit stand firm in Christ. The power is to establish ourselves as well as edify others.

This passage introduces two new and meaningful aspects of Spirit baptism. It is a 'seal' and a 'deposit'.

The most common use of seals in the ancient world was as a mark of ownership: 'This property is mine.' How significant that this should be a metaphor for baptism in Spirit. When the promised gift is given, God himself is saying: 'This person is mine.' It is quite literally a 'confirmation'. One cannot but recall Jesus' own reception of the Spirit, accompanied by words from heaven: 'This is my Son, whom I love; with him I am well pleased' (Matt. 3:17).

It is of the essence of a seal that it can be clearly observed by others. In Jesus' case, the dove was seen by at least one other (John) and the voice was heard by a large crowd, though some mistook it for thunder. We have noticed in Acts that when anyone was baptised in Spirit, not only did they know it but anyone else present was also fully aware that it had happened. The evidence was audible and visible.

The 'deposit' is simply the first instalment, a visible token of much more to come later. It can either be the first instalment of goods bought or the first payment for them. It is always a sample; what will follow is more of the same. Baptism in Spirit is a foretaste of all that is to come. For example, one result is physical, a vigour in our mortal bodies (Rom. 8:11) which is an anticipation of the resurrection with a new immortal body, created by the power of the same Spirit (Rom. 1:4; 1 Cor. 15:53-4). The praise released in Spirit baptism is a glimpse of worship in heaven.

While it is a pledge of all this, it needs to be said that Spirit baptism is not a guarantee that we shall have it all.

The New International Version boldly adds a complete phrase that is not in the original text: 'guaranteeing what is to come', but at least the translators did not go so far as to add 'to us' at the end. The 'deposit' does guarantee *what* is to come, but not *who* it will come to. Too many believers want a guarantee against themselves – that whatever they later do or don't do, they will still get it all. Inheritance depends on perseverance (both 'Calvinists' and 'Arminians' agree on this). It is those who 'overcome' who inherit the new heaven and earth (Rev. 21:7).

Finally, note the word 'anointed', another synonym for receiving the 'oil' of the Spirit.

Galatians 3:2 'Did you receive the Spirit by observing the law, or by believing what you heard?' It is a rhetorical question, but Paul expects his readers to think of the answer and is absolutely confident what that will be – a confirmation that God's gifts are received through faith, not by attempting to keep his commandments (remember the Spirit was first given at Pentecost, the very anniversary of the law being given to Moses at Sinai).

The main reason for quoting this here relates to the question, 'How did Paul expect them to know that they "received the Spirit"?' (the same question that arose in connection with Acts 19:2). They could not appeal to the New Testament because they didn't have it yet (nor could they know that the letter they were reading would be part of it). There can really be only one explanation. Paul expected them to answer directly from their experience at the time, not by deduction from anything that happened later. The aorist tense of the verb 'receive' points to that initial event, although he then goes on to ask a similar question about the continued supply of the Spirit, of which they have also been fully aware because the power to 'work miracles' was the evidence (3:5), again the result of believing, not keeping the law.

Both the initial reception and continual supply of the Spirit were *self-evident experiences*. That is the clear implication of this passage.

Ephesians 1:13b-14 'Having believed, you were marked in him with a seal, the promised Holy Spirit, who is a deposit of our inheritance until the redemption of those who are God's possession' (the NIV again inserts 'guaranteeing', which is not original). Here we have the same combination of 'seal' and 'deposit' ('earnest' translates the Greek word *arrabon* in older versions). We have already commented on both (when we looked at 2 Cor. 1:21-2). 'Promised' reminds us of Peter's preaching at Pentecost (Acts 2:33, 39).

'Having believed' is worth noting. We have come across this exact same word (Greek *pisteusantes*) twice before (in John 7:39 and Acts 19:2). In both those, 'believing' and 'receiving' were separated, in content and chronology. One followed the other. The same is indicated here, as the tense of the verb indicates. Having (already) believed, they were (then) sealed. Whether the seal was given immediately after or later is not relevant. But it is seen by Paul as an element in their initiation.

'Until the redemption' points to the fact that for Paul the process of salvation is far from complete for any believer. He uses the verb 'saved' in three tenses, past, present and future – we have been saved, we are being saved and we will be saved. If anything, he emphasises the last more than the other two. Our salvation will be complete when our bodies are finally redeemed (Rom. 8:23); in that same verse he talks about those 'who have the firstfruits of the Spirit [equivalent to the deposit] groaning and longing' for this consummation. The gift of the Spirit is only a fraction of our full salvation. It seals our departure on 'the Way' of salvation; it does not mean that we have 'arrived' at our destination. The same link between the seal and our future redemption recurs later (Eph. 4:30).

Ephesians 5:18 'Do not get drunk on wine, which leads to debauchery. Instead, be filled with the Spirit.'

This verse is so often interpreted as an exhortation to turn away from sin and pursue holiness. Certainly the wider context of the whole chapter is concerned with this. But this verse could have a simpler application as guidance for believers when they want to hold a celebration, when they want to 'have a good time'. The succeeding verses describe a sing-song, not a superior state of sanctification! Alcohol can produce this, but there is a price to pay, a moral (or rather, an immoral) hangover. The Spirit can also stimulate this, without any of the bad results.

Most preachers and teachers make much of the present

tense of the second verb: '*Go on* being filled in Spirit' (the preposition is *en* again). The point of including this verse here is quite simple. How can anyone go on being filled if they've never once been filled? And isn't that first filling the same as being 'baptised in Spirit' (as in Acts 2:4)?

2 Timothy 1:6-7 'For this reason I remind you to fan into flame the gift of God, which is in you through the laying on of my hands. For God did not give us a spirit of timidity, but a Spirit of power, of love and of self-discipline.'

There can be little doubt that Paul is referring to Timothy's baptism in Spirit. We know that Paul laid hands on his converts after their baptism in water for this very purpose. Verse 7 is clearly an amplified description of the gifts of the Spirit and has clear echoes of his other contrast between a slavish fear and the bold intimacy of an adopted son (Rom. 8:15). Here, the comparison takes a milder form – between timidity and confidence. Timothy is Paul's adopted son as well as God's. 'Power' refers to the gifts of the Spirit, whereas 'love' and 'self-control' are the fruit (though the last is a different word from that used in Galatians 5:23 and could be translated as 'sound judgment').

In his first letter to Timothy, Paul makes a similar exhortation: 'Do not neglect your gift, which was given you through a prophetic message when the body of elders laid hands on you' (1 Tim. 4:14). Some have thought that this refers to the same occasion. But this was at the hands of a group of elders, not necessarily including Paul, and probably happened when he was set apart to teach and pastor a particular church or group of churches. 'Gift' in this case would be a particular equipping for this task, a gift *from* the Spirit, after he had received the gift *of* the Spirit at the hands of Paul.

However, both the gift of the Spirit and the later gifting from the Spirit need to be constantly experienced and exercised. An untended fire will go out and a neglected gift will atrophy, like unused muscles. Baptism in Spirit and subsequent gifts are only a beginning. Both need to be 'stirred up', if they are not to 'die down'.

Titus 3:5b-7 'He saved us through the washing [or bath] of rebirth and renewal by Holy Spirit, whom he poured out on us generously through Jesus Christ our Saviour, so that, having been justified by his grace, we might become heirs having the hope of eternal life.'

This verse seems to echo John 3:5 in more ways than one. 'Washing' and 'Spirit' are close to 'water and Spirit'; many commentators find a reference to baptism here as well as there. 'Born' is the same root word, though here combined with 'again' (*palin*), whereas there it was 'from above' (*anothen*). There are also echoes of Acts 2:33, particularly in the verb 'poured out'. The addition here of the adverb 'generously' (or 'copiously') underlines the overwhelming nature of the experience, making it more difficult to believe that it could have happened unconsciously, without them being aware of it. There are three significant features in Paul's statement.

First, the biblical use of the word 'renewal' is used of the very beginning of the Christian life, for that 'new creation' which is true of anyone who is in Christ (2 Cor. 5:17). It is not used of any later development, much less a change in the condition of a church.

Second, Paul confidently uses 'pentecostal terminology' of all his 'saved' readers, without qualification or exception. This is yet another confirmation that baptism in Spirit, as described in Acts, was extended to all believers in the early Church and was the normal start in Christian living, an initial rather than a subsequent experience.

Third, those who limit the significance of Spirit baptism to 'power for service' and see no connection with salvation must be puzzled, if not challenged to rethink their position, by the direct dependence of the 'outpoured Spirit' on the verb 'saved' in this sentence. Not surprisingly, they rarely refer to this passage when teaching on this subject.

This concludes our studies in the Pauline Epistles.

Non-Pauline Other writers tend to use other synonyms or make indirect references. These need to be understood in the light of our findings so far.

John Like his Gospel compared to the Synoptics, John's letter contains more material on the Holy Spirit than other Epistles. The most important texts for our purpose tend to use the simpler terms: 'given' and 'received', though 'anointing' is another of his words (1 John 2:27).

'And this is how we know that he [God] lives in us: We know it by the Spirit he gave us' (3:24b). 'Know' is a key word; it is used thirty-six times in this short letter. John wants his readers to be sure of their salvation. The Spirit is the source of this certainty. Receiving the Spirit given by God is a self-evident event and experience. However, this initial 'confirmation' needs to be backed up later by the testimony of a good conscience and love for brethren in the church.

The 'anointing' received at the beginning remains to give a double discernment when listening to teaching (2:27) and when teaching others (4:6), because 'the Spirit of truth' is in them.

There is an unusual combination of three witnesses to the truth about the Son of God – 'the Spirit, the water and the blood' (5:7). We have already come across the witness of the Spirit (in Romans 8:15), but to what do the 'water' and 'blood' refer? John says that Jesus 'came through' these, perhaps referring to the baptism (in water) that began his ministry and the baptism (in fire) that ended it, with the shedding of his blood on the cross. John actually saw the extraordinary flow of 'blood and water' from Jesus' side when a soldier pierced his heart with a spear to make sure he was dead (a symptom of a ruptured pericardium or a 'broken heart'; crucifixion by itself would not kill a man in six hours unless his legs were broken).

The aspect of the given Spirit most important to John

is not purity, power or unity, but truth. He testifies to the truth about the Saviour and the truth about those he is saving. In both the Hebrew and the Greek languages, 'truth' and 'reality' are the same word and are therefore interchangeable in English. Believers need a firm grasp of both objective and subjective realities of faith.

Hebrews The only relevant passage is where the unknown author lists the first steps of the Christian life as 'repentance from acts that lead to death, and of faith in God, instruction about baptisms, the laying on of hands' (6:1b-2a).

That the last phrase refers to the prayerful practice of seeking baptism in Spirit seems to be indicated by his succeeding description of those who have responded to these 'elementary teachings'. They have 'been enlightened, tasted the heavenly gift, become sharers in Holy Spirit, tasted the goodness of the word of God and the powers of the coming age' (6:4-5). It is a good summary of those who have been baptised in Spirit.

Notice the order in the teaching they have received: repentance, faith, baptism, then prayer for the Spirit. This seems to have been the normal sequence in experience as well as in instruction.

As most know, the author is urging them to go on from this, to grow up and mature (6:1). He is also warning them that it could all be lost, never to be recovered (6:6-8), though he is optimistic that this will not be the case for them (6:9-12).

Revelation In one sense, this book is quite a different kind of literature – 'apocalyptic' (which means 'unveiling', usually of the future, hence often in pictorial symbolism). But the book is in the form of a circular letter to seven churches in Asia, so it is convenient to include it here, among the Epistles, rather than to start another section.

In any case, there is very little in it that is relevant to our study. We need only point to the invitation twice given in its final pages. The thirsty are invited to 'drink the water of life as a free gift without cost' (21:6b; 22:17b; an echo of Isaiah 55:1a). Since the offer is addressed to those still living in this world, the 'water of life' is surely the same as the 'living water' which the same Jesus speaking in this book offered earlier to the thirsty, as recorded by the same apostle to whom he gave his 'revelation' (John 4:14; 7:37).

We have completed our studies in the New Testament. For your comfort, let me say that this is by far the longest and perhaps the meatiest chapter in the book! I hope you'll find it easier going from now on.

As I have reread what I've written, I have been struck by the number of times I have questioned modern English translations, particularly the New International Version. This is the one I mainly use, partly because it can be read aloud to others so easily and so meaningfully, which I love doing and find as effective as preaching. It deserves its nickname – the Nearly Infallible Version! Yet I have had occasion to criticise the translation of a considerable number of verses connected with our theme, often giving my own version of the original text. I wonder what readers will make of this.

Some may well think I am both arrogant and impudent to question the achievements and even the integrity of such eminent and dedicated translators. Others may jump to the conclusion that I am simply twisting scriptures to suit myself, because they don't fit my theory. That is certainly a temptation of which I am only too aware.

However, I dare to say this: don't believe any of my comments about 'the original text' until you have checked them all out for yourself. If you know elementary Greek, that will be easy – just get hold of a Greek New Testament. Or you could find someone else who knows the language, maybe your pastor, and ask for a little of their time. Even without any Greek, you could beg, borrow or buy an interlinear Greek-English New Testament, which puts the English words directly beneath the Greek. You can see most of my 'corrections' at a glance – for example, the presence or absence of the definite article 'the'. I am confident enough to believe that most, if not all, of my claims will be seen to be valid.

This raises an important question. Why should translators of ability and integrity make so many 'mistakes', or at least overlook so many subtle features and nuances? The fact that these slips are largely confined to the very verses we have been studying gives us a clue. Three factors have influenced them (whether consciously or unconsciously God alone knows, but I suspect it could be a mixture of varying proportions).

First, I would guess that many if not most of the

translators have not had a personal experience of the baptism in Spirit, such as we have been finding. They have therefore been working in the dark to some degree. Only someone who has had that experience can come to these passages with that personal knowledge and understanding of what they are describing.

Second, translators are not without their own theology, shaped by the tradition from which they come and their own thinking. For example, it is unlikely that a translator will write 'baptised *in* water', if he was sprinkled as a baby; he will prefer 'with'.

Third, not unrelated to this, translators are aware of the traditions held by the churches in which they hope their version will be accepted and used. This is why the word 'baptise' (Greek *baptizo*) is transliterated and never translated. To put 'dip', 'plunge' or 'immerse' would lower sales in most Western denominations! So more ambiguous expressions are used, to avoid giving offence ('baptism *with* water' covers everything – except the baptised!). Funnily enough, the general secretary of the Bible Society told me that most 'foreign' scriptures *do* translate the word into a colloquial equivalent (perhaps because adult baptism by immersion is so much more common on the mission field).

These reservations over freely translating verses relating to water baptism spill over (sorry, another pun!) into those relating to Spirit baptism, compounding the problem. We shall have more to say about this when we discuss the practical problems (in Chapter 7).

Meanwhile, there are other matters to discuss. We

have been pulling passages apart for long enough. It is time to be putting things together.

4

The Doctrinal Definition

Analysis must give way to synthesis. Having pulled apart the New Testament data we must now put it all together, but in a different form. We must attempt a systematic summary of what all these passages teach about baptism in Spirit, preferably with an outline that can be easily remembered.

It has been said that if you ask the right questions, you don't need the answers but can work them out for yourself. There is some truth in this, so I am going to build this chapter around the four basic questions – who, how, when and why?

To each of these questions I shall give two complementary answers, using alliteration (in this case, both words beginning with the same letter), a further aid to the memory. These sub-headings will cover the eight distinctive aspects we have found in our study of the relevant texts.

It will perhaps help to mention at this point that one fundamental premise underlies this whole chapter, namely the equation we have earlier established – that 'receiving' and 'being baptised' in the Spirit are one and the same thing. Unless the reader is by now convinced of this, the doctrine about to be defined will be equally unconvincing. The implications of this one assumption reach into every other aspect.

WHO?

This is really two separate questions – who baptises in Spirit and who is baptised in Spirit? We shall deal with them accordingly.

Baptiser Who is the baptiser in Spirit? The answer could not be clearer. Jesus is the one and only agent able to do this. He is the baptiser. It is part of his 'ascension' ministry after returning home to his Father in heaven. John emphatically said this and so did Peter on the day of Pentecost.

However, both the Gospels and Acts make it quite clear that the Spirit is received by Jesus before he pours out the Spirit on anyone else. Actually, he received the Spirit twice, for himself at the Jordan river and for others at the throne of God. Therefore the reception of the Spirit by others can be seen as the gift of God, as the apostle John tends to see it, in answer to the prayer of Jesus.

This does not mean that it always happens without human assistance. The prayer of others may be involved and the laying on of hands may be a channel of impartation as well as an intense form of intercession. But there is no hint of those who already possess the Spirit passing the Spirit on to others.

Jesus himself is always actively involved in every baptism in Spirit. Anyone can baptise in water but he, and he alone, is the baptiser in Spirit every time.

Believers Who is baptised in Spirit? The world (of unbelievers) cannot receive the Spirit. There are necessary qualifications to be met before this can happen. Two are absolutely essential, a third is usually required and a fourth may be needed.

The two basic preconditions are true repentance towards God for sins committed (including deeds proving this; Luke 3:8; Acts 26:20) and personal faith in Jesus Christ as Saviour and Lord. Only such penitent believers can expect to be 'confirmed' by the gift of the Spirit.

The one usually required is baptism in water. God is obviously free to override this in exceptional circumstances, but we are not. The gospel is to be obeyed and baptism is one of the first acts of that obedience (Matt. 28:19; Acts 2:38). We have seen that the normal sequence is for Spirit baptism to follow upon water baptism.

The one that may well be needed is prayer, by the recipients themselves or others seeking to help them, with or without the laying on of hands. There is no command in scripture to suggest this is the only way but there is more than a suggestion that it is the right course to take if there is a delay in receiving.

Other preconditions have been added in church tradition, for which there is no warrant. Some of these are subjective – for example, a high degree of 'consecration' or sanctification. But these are usually associated with mistaken 'second blessing' ideas. Others are objective – for example, that the Spirit can only be given at the hands of bishops in an 'apostolic succession' (a sequence of physical contact going right back to the apostles!). We need to return to the simplicity of the apostolic requirements.

HOW?

Here we are almost entirely dependent on the descriptions in Acts, though there are hints elsewhere. How is anybody baptised in Spirit? What exactly happens, if anything? How does anyone know it has happened to them, or to someone else? Is there any immediate result, or does this only appear later? These are the kinds of question people ask, and they deserve a clear answer.

Experience One scholar sums it up by pointing out that in scripture baptism in Spirit was always 'a definite, even dramatic, experience'. Another says it was 'as definite as catching influenza'.

In other words, it is a self-evident event, of which both the recipient and any others are fully aware. This is the inescapable conclusion from a study of Acts. Paul expected 'disciples' to know when or whether this had happened to them (Acts 19:2; Gal. 3:2).

The language used ('drenched in', 'falling upon', 'poured out upon', 'filled with') carries the clear implication that it is an experience of which one is fully conscious. It is very significant that those who believe it can happen to a person without him or her realising it never use this kind of language. It would be very inappropriate. This omission is conspicuous in those who claim that 'believing' and 'receiving' are one and the same thing.

The same teachers tend to add that we must believe we *have* received what we ask for, whether there is any discernible result or not. They often quote Jesus: 'Therefore I tell you, whatever you ask for in prayer, believe that you have received it, and it will be yours' (Mark 11:24). They seem not to notice the subtle change in the future tense in that last clause: not 'it is already yours' but 'it *will be* yours'. If I pray for ten pounds, I need to believe my prayer is heard and the money is already on its way. But I will know for sure when it reaches me. I have prayed for a number to receive the Spirit, assured them the prayer has been heard and made them promise to tell me when it happens. I do not encourage them to 'believe' it has before it has!

So how do they, and others, know when it has? Is it as clear as having the ten pounds in your hand?

Evidence We are passing from the internal experience (for which 'filled' is as good a word as any) to the outward evidence. Again, we must start with Acts, in which we find a consistent pattern. The clause 'what you now see and hear' points to visible and audible phenomena which invariably accompany baptism in Spirit.

All the recorded occasions point to unexpected speech,

spontaneously ejaculated. After all, Jesus taught that whatever the heart was filled with would emerge from the mouth (which is why we will be judged for our careless words; Matt. 12:36). What kind of speech is unmistakable evidence that a person has been 'filled' with Holy Spirit?

'Tongues' for a start (horrid word!). Fluent speech in a language never before either learned or spoken is obviously a supernatural endowment. This is the most common evidence mentioned and should not be treated with suspicion or contempt. It can encourage people to believe that the Spirit enables them to go beyond their natural ability, leading them into other 'spiritual gifts' (Greek *charismata*, from which 'charismatic' is derived).

But to insist that it must always be such 'tongues' is to be narrower than scripture. While it may be more frequent than any other form of inspired speech, that does not warrant the demand that it *must* be this gift, as *the* 'initial evidence'. Other 'overflows' are mentioned – for example, 'praise' and 'prophecy', both of which are in a known and familiar language.

On the other hand, many understand the evidence in much too broad a manner, reaching the point where almost anything they fancy will do! Others do not believe in immediate evidence but look for ultimate results, like 'fruit of the Spirit' (love, joy, peace, etc.), but this appears gradually and much later and is more difficult to measure.

The scripture puts the emphasis on simultaneous

evidence, which is always verbal, a fulfilment of the prediction (in Joel) that all would 'prophesy'.

I cannot say too strongly that the biblical record totally ignores any physical or emotional changes of state, even if these did accompany the event (which we have no way of knowing). Such behaviour in other contexts is interpreted as reactions of the human spirit to an unexpected encounter with a supernatural presence, but never seen as actions of the Holy Spirit (see my book, *Is the Blessing Biblical?*, Hodder and Stoughton, 1995, which examines the 'Toronto' phenomena).

To sum up, some form of spontaneous inspired speech seems to strike the biblical balance, of which 'tongues' may be the most frequent.

WHEN?

This is one of the most critical issues and the major reason for the division between the charismatic and pentecostal streams on the one hand and the sacramental and evangelical streams on the other (this will be explained in detail in Chapter 5).

Does baptism in Spirit take place at the time of conversion or is it 'subsequent' to that? Is it a 'first' or a 'second' blessing? Even more bluntly, is it an introduction to ordinary Christian living or does it lift a Christian to a higher level?

Our findings have already indicated the answer we shall give here. It is two-fold, individual and corporate.

Initiation   Baptism in Spirit is part and parcel of becoming a Christian. It belongs to the beginning of the Christian life. It is the first and only 'reception' of the Spirit, without which Christian living would be impossible.

Baptism in water and baptism in Spirit belong together, though they are never synonymous and never simultaneous. Either without the other is inadequate to give disciples a proper start. If either was missing, or even both, the apostles took immediate steps to remedy the deficiency. They did not waste time discussing the spiritual state or status of the deficient (e.g. would they still go to heaven if they died before getting everything?); that is a modern curiosity that reveals more interest in the minimum admission fee for heaven than the maximum acceptance of a saved life on earth.

Furthermore, in the New Testament the Spirit is not considered to 'indwell' believers until he has been 'received' – that is, until they have been 'baptised'. Until then, the relationship with the Spirit must be somewhat like that of the first disciples – he is 'with' them (convicting them of sin, helping them to repent and believe), but not yet 'in' them (more of this in Chapter 7).

To say that baptism in Spirit belongs to initiation does not mean that there cannot be a considerable lapse of time between 'believing' and 'receiving'. We have found three very different sequences in Acts, two of which are unusual, if not abnormal, while one seems to be the average, or normal, pattern.

In the case of the first disciples and the Samaritans,

there was a considerable delay, for one reason or another. This was clearly abnormal and cannot be regarded as a precedent (pentecostals have used Acts 1 to justify 'waiting meetings', but the 120 *had* to wait until God's chosen day of Pentecost).

At the other extreme, it is very hard to distinguish 'believing' and 'receiving' in the case of Cornelius and his household, especially since they 'received' before being baptised and even before the preacher had really started on his sermon (note 'as I began to speak' in Acts 11:15). This, too, was abnormal, though we can guess why it was. It was never repeated, so far as we know.

Long intervals and no interval seem to be abnormal. A quite short one appears normal, as in Acts 19, where they believed before and received the Spirit shortly after being baptised. Other scriptures confirm this sequence (e.g. Heb. 6:2). This close association in time explains the usage of 'having believed [Greek *pisteusantes*], you received' – both as a question and a statement.

Incorporation   One thing is agreed by all: to be 'in Christ' is to be in his body, the Church. But when does anyone come to be 'in Christ'? Does that happen when a person first believes, as both evangelicals and pentecostals would hold? If so, what are we to make of the phrase 'baptised into Christ' (Gal. 3:27), which appears to make water baptism the point of entry into the Church, as most sacramentalists would hold? Both views have to grapple with the clearest statement of all (1 Cor. 12:13), which makes baptism in Spirit the moment of being incorporated 'into one body'. As we have seen, both views get round the problem by saying that 'baptism in Spirit' is one and the same thing as being baptised (the sacramental solution) or believing (the evangelical solution). But we have been at pains to point out that in the New Testament Spirit baptism is clearly distinguished, theologically and chronologically, from both believing and water baptism. So how can we resolve the dilemma?

The first thing to say is that, in those days, all three (believing, being baptised and receiving) were so closely associated, both in time and in their thinking, that they were considered together rather than separately, aspects of the same initiation, a kind of experiential 'trinity'. The disciples would probably be puzzled by our modern debates. Had we asked them which of the three steps incorporated them into Christ, they would probably have been astonished by the question and replied: 'Why, all three, of course!'

Whereas we, in our enlightened age (!), have separated them so widely, in time and therefore in thought, that we set them over against each other, debating whether it is belief or baptism, water baptism or Spirit baptism, that brings us into Christ's body. Belief and baptism are widely separated, not just in 'paedobaptist' circles where babies are 'done', but also in 'credobaptist' circles where believers are 'done'. Baptism comes either long before belief or some considerable time after. Contemporary evangelism rarely counsels enquirers, as Peter did, 'Repent and be baptised, every one of you, in the name of Jesus Christ, so that your sins may be forgiven'

(Acts 2:38). Evangelists talking like this today would lose most of their church support.

Similarly, water baptism and Spirit baptism have become widely separated, whereas in the apostolic days they invariably followed one another, with water usually first. Even 'credobaptist' churches rarely lay hands on the baptised and pray that they may receive the Spirit. They have probably already been told that they got the Spirit when they 'received Jesus'!

Until we get all these elements in initiation back together again, the confusion over exactly *when* incorporation into the body occurs will remain an unnecessary but inevitable division of opinion. However, there is a helpful and perhaps reconciling undertone to the key statement (in 1 Cor. 12:13). Here the verb 'baptise' is qualified by the two prepositions 'in' and 'into'. There is a precedent for this in John's statement about baptism in water, which is 'into' repentance (Matt. 3:11). Yet John demanded repentance, indeed 'fruits of repentance', *before* he would baptise anyone 'into repentance' (Luke 3:8). So baptism was the climax and consummation of what was already happening in their lives. It was a 'seal' on their repentance, a final farewell to the sins they had confessed and made restitution for. We could apply this same principle to baptism in Spirit. Believing and being baptised in water have played a part in bringing a person into Christ and his body, but baptism in Spirit brings this process to its proper conclusion, 'sealing' them into his body. The reason why this 'gradual' progression into the body is widely rejected in favour of a 'sudden' – even instantaneous – entry is because it has been linked too strongly with future security rather than present salvation and service. There is more interest in being 'safe from hell' than 'saved from sins'. There is a demand to be part of the Church as quickly as possible, to make sure of getting a ticket to heaven. The result is that many regard water and Spirit baptism as optional extras when it comes to salvation and cannot relate either to being 'saved', though scripture clearly does (e.g. Mark 16:16; 1 Pet. 3:21; Titus 3:5).

What we can say is that baptism in Spirit *fully* integrates believers 'into the body' of Christ, by releasing in them those gifts which will enable them to function as true 'members' of a body. We have already explained the difference between this and membership of a club, between a role and a roll. The whole chapter (1 Cor. 12) is based on the premise that because *all* have been baptised in one Spirit, *each* has received a 'spiritual gift' to use for the benefit of *every* other member of the same body.

The Church is the 'fellowship' of the Holy Spirit. This word (Greek *koinonia*) means far more than having a discussion followed by tea and biscuits. It is used of Siamese twins sharing the same bloodstream, or partners in a business whose financial fortunes will rise or fall together. It is mutual interdependence to a very high degree. The life of the church is the life of the same Spirit coursing through each and every member. Without baptism in Spirit, the life is simply not there. The church may still have a reputation for being 'alive', because of lively activity, but in reality it is dead (like the church in Sardis; Rev. 3:1).

But we are jumping ahead, from when to why, so let's look at that now.

WHY?

To answer the overall question as to why we need the Holy Spirit would require a much larger book than this, to include an exposition of every text in the whole New Testament mentioning his work, of which there are many aspects. The reason we are considering the purpose of baptism in Spirit here is because of the quite sharp division between evangelicals, who see it largely in terms of salvation, and pentecostals, who see it exclusively in terms of service. To put it another way: who benefits most when people are baptised in Spirit, themselves or others? Does it primarily help them to be saved or others to be served?

This is yet another example of Luke and Paul being set over against each other. Acts is said to be exclusively concerned with power for service (actually, that's only true of references to the day of Pentecost). The Epistles, especially those of Paul, are said to concentrate on personal salvation (actually, 1 Corinthians 12-14 is all about service to others). So a false alternative is created and an unnecessary choice has to be made.

Why does it have to be either/or? Why can't it be both/and? They are neither incompatible nor mutually exclusive. I believe the New Testament holds both in a proper balance. We are 'saved to serve'.

Salvation There are immediate objections to a link between baptism in Spirit and salvation, usually expressed in an emotive challenge: 'Are you saying that those who have not been baptised in Spirit are not saved?!' The same indignant protest is made about water baptism. Of course, the question is already 'loaded' with a particular understanding of 'saved', usually related to hell rather than sins, conceived as an instantaneous event rather than an extended process and morbidly concerned with what happens if a person dies without it rather than lives without it. I have found that the simplest way to answer these questions is to ask one in return (as Jesus often did): 'Saved from what?' That questions the faulty premise of the question – an inadequate definition of 'saved'.

Then I add that neither the apostles nor the believers in the early Church would ever have dreamed of asking such a question. If Jesus is to be Lord of our lives, whatever he demands (water baptism) and whatever he offers (Spirit baptism) is essential for anyone who calls him 'Lord'. That went without saying in the early days. Who are we to ask whether we can still be 'saved' without complying with his will and wishes? This 'minimum admission' mentality explains a great deal of the contrast between the ancient and modern Church.

We have had frequent occasion to note the use of the concept 'saved' in the context of baptism in Spirit ('saved by grace' in Acts 15:11; 'washed . . . in the Spirit of God' in 1 Cor. 6:11; 'saved through . . . renewal of outpoured Spirit' in Titus 3:5).

Salvation is a process composed of three phases,

expressed in past, present and future tenses in scripture. We 'have been saved' from the penalty of sin (justification). We 'are being saved' from the power of sin (sanctification). We 'will be saved' from the pollution of sin (glorification). Baptism in Spirit directly relates to all three.

It is the *proof of justification*. We are justified, declared innocent in God's court and acquitted when we repent of our sins and believe in the Saviour. But how can anyone *know* that their sins are forgiven, that God has accepted them and adopted them as his sons? There are two approaches to this need for 'assurance'.

One is induction from scripture. 'The Bible says it, you believe it, that settles it.' This 'syllogism', as such logic reasoning is called, is based on head knowledge. But an active brain can produce doubts which ask probing questions: have I repented and believed *enough* to ensure that the logic applies to me personally? This rational basis for assurance is not found in the New Testament, which reveals a rather different approach.

The other is immersion in Spirit. This assurance is for the heart, not the head. It is a direct testimony to the spirit, rather than indirect logical argument.

Peter argued (in Acts 10, 11 and 15) that he had proof of God's acceptance of the Gentiles in their being given the Spirit, in the *same* way as everybody else. Paul describes a continuous witness of the divine Spirit to the human spirit (Rom. 8:15). John says we know we are sons of God because he has given us his Spirit (1 John 3:24; 4:13).

The gift of the Spirit, then, is the proof, the evidence

of sins forgiven and acceptance with God. It is the divine 'confirmation' of our sonship, as it was for Jesus himself. That is why the word 'seal' is used of the Spirit. His coming settles it.

This is not to say that a person cannot be justified or have their sins forgiven without baptism in Spirit. That would be against all the texts supporting 'justification by faith'. Sins are forgiven when repented of and confessed. What we are saying is that no one can be *certain* of all this until the gift of the Spirit makes it absolutely sure and the continued witness of the Spirit maintains that assurance.

Of course, baptism in Spirit can only be such a proof, such a 'seal', if it is a clearly defined self-evident experience; otherwise it becomes too vague to fulfil this function.

It is the *prerequisite of sanctification*. We are saved 'to' as well as 'from', to holiness as well as from sinfulness. Salvation is positive as well as negative and will not be complete until we are fully restored to the image of God and the likeness of Christ, which will happen when we see him face to face (1 John 3:2).

But it is utterly impossible for us to achieve holiness in our own strength, as many who have tried know only too well. All their efforts and exertions end in hypocritical pride or humiliating despair. We can never achieve it by our own power. We need supernatural power. We need holy power. We need holy Spirit. We need to be drenched in holy Spirit.

This is exactly how John the baptiser meant 'you shall

be baptised in holy Spirit' to be understood. His whole message centred on the need for purity, not the need for power. This baptism would meet the needs of those baptised rather than the needs of others, in his mind and message.

How could anyone live a holy life without being soaked in holy Spirit first? God's standards are too high for us to reach unless he helps us. There is an alarming recent development which calls God's laws his 'ideals' (e.g. heterosexuality is his 'ideal'; homosexuality is not his 'ideal'), a very misleading word which suggests that we cannot hope to reach them but will be accepted for having aimed in their direction! God demands of his people, Jewish or Christian, that they 'be holy as he is holy' (Lev. 19:1; 1 Pet. 1:16). God doesn't lower his standards to meet people; he lifts people to meet his standards – by giving them his holy Spirit.

The New Testament introduces us to the 'fruit' of the Spirit: love, joy and peace in God; patience, kindness and goodness to others; faithfulness, meekness and self-control in ourselves. These are not nine fruits but one fruit with nine flavours, which all grow together or not at all (unbelievers can only produce three or four at most, depending on their temperament). From another point of view, the whole fruit is seen perfectly in Jesus. The Spirit's fruit in us reproduces his character. Holiness is Christlikeness. Another word is 'fullness', though the noun is not used. Those who have matured in purity are said to be 'full of Spirit' (Acts 6:3; but note that it also means power – 6:8).

Not that the gift of the Spirit makes human effort obsolete. His resources must be constantly appropriated and applied. 'Make every effort . . . to be holy; without holiness no-one will see the Lord' (Heb. 12:14). It is a co-operative effort and it is now infinitely worthwhile because the goal can be achieved.

One final word here. Some have seen baptism in Spirit as the end of the process of sanctification rather than its beginning, even giving it the label of 'entire sanctific- ation' (we shall say more about the 'Holiness' movements and denominations in the next chapter). Needless to say, they also insist that it must be a subsequent or 'second' blessing given only to mature and dedicated believers after long seeking. Our studies have not validated this view. The Holy Spirit is given at the beginning of the Christian life, to help us, to enable us to grow in holiness as we walk in the Spirit. It is a false expectation to assume baptism in holy Spirit will immediately produce 'entire sanctification' and it is a mistaken judgment to criticise Spirit baptism because those receiving it are not immediately holy. It is also wrong for the 'baptised' to imagine that suddenly they are more mature or holy, superior to those without the experience. Some believers who have not 'received' can be more faithful and devoted to the Lord than some who have. But the former would be even better if they had 'received' and the latter might be a good deal worse if they hadn't! The Lord will judge us by what use we have made of the resources we have had (as the two parables of the wise and foolish bridesmaids and the talents given to the servants both illustrate; Matt. 25:1-30).

The view that baptism in Spirit begins a life set free from all selfishness and sinfulness, with a heart of 'perfect love' for God and man, became so strong in the nineteenth century that we need to underline here the absence of scriptural basis for this assumption. If, as we have seen, *all* believers in the early Church received Spirit baptism, they should then have been 'entirely sanctified'. This would make obsolete most of the Epistles of the New Testament. Those written to Corinth and Galatia don't assume that their readers are 'entirely sanctified'. So baptism in Spirit doesn't sanctify us, make us holy, in itself. But he, when he has come to indwell us, makes it gloriously possible, if we respond rightly to this invasion of holy power.

It is the *promise of glorification*. Baptism in Spirit is not just a taste of holiness; it is a taste of heaven. It is an experience of the 'powers of the age to come', for those who have 'shared in the Holy Spirit' (Heb. 6:5).

It is an eschatological experience, a bit of the age to come penetrating this present age. It is a sign that the 'last days' (Acts 2:17) are upon us, that the final era of human history has begun.

But it is also the 'deposit', the first instalment of what 'no eye has seen, no ear has heard, no mind has conceived – what God has prepared for those who love him' (1 Cor. 2:9, quoting Isa. 64:4).

This is why praise, poetry and music have been associated with being 'Spirit-filled'. It is the language of heaven, of which there are many examples in the book of Revelation. Singing, shouting and clapping hands are all released in the Spirit, as in the Psalms of David, on whom the Spirit remained.

Above all, the Spirit is the first down-payment of the future resurrection, the redemption of our bodies (2 Cor. 5:1-5). His was the power that raised Jesus from the dead in a 'glorious body' (Rom. 1:4) and it is by the same power that we shall don our immortal bodies (1 Cor. 15:53; Phil. 3:21).

And beyond that lies the new heaven and the new earth. As the Spirit was the executive power of the Godhead in the first creation (Gen. 1:2), he will surely be the same at 'the renewal of all things' (Matt. 19:28).

So baptism in Spirit is the proof of justification, the pre-requisite of sanctification and the promise of glorification. If that does not tie the experience to salvation, I don't know what else would.

Service Yes, we are saved to serve. Baptism in Spirit is for the benefit of others, as well as ourselves. We are called to be holy and we are called to be witnesses. The Spirit supplies the power for both. Luke's and Paul's writings both emphasise 'power for service', but with different perspectives – which are complementary rather than contradictory.

Paul focuses on service inside the Church, building her up ('edifying' is his word, like 'edifice') in *quality*. Baptism in Spirit releases gifts in every member, which benefit the whole body. Of these 'spiritual gifts' (Greek *charismata*, called by Catholic scholars 'grace-gifts', a very good translation), only 'tongues' can be used to edify oneself (1 Cor. 14:4), but only when it is 'interpreted', i.e. translated into a familiar language, does it edify anyone else (1 Cor. 14:5). All the others benefit someone else. A gift of healing is not given to make the healer special but to keep others healthy. Luke would not disagree with this. In most of his reports on baptism in Spirit it is seen as a normal part of becoming a Christian and joining the Church.

Luke, however, focuses on service outside the body, building the Church up in *quantity*. It is the power to witness that is his primary interest, the spread of the gospel. He emphasises 'boldness' of speech (*parresia*) even more than tongues (*glossolalia*) in his record (Acts 4:13,29,31). But the power is to be seen as well as heard, particularly in the 'signs' of exorcising demons and healing diseases, the two most common symptoms of Satan's kingdom. There will be more spectacular miracles as well – raising the dead (Acts 10:40), escape from prison (12:10; 16:26), shipwreck (27:27-44) and venomous snakes (28:3-6). All this was 'power evangelism', as it has been called today, and fulfilled Jesus' promise that his followers would be able to repeat his miracles (John 14:12). 'Miraculous powers' are also listed by Paul as one of the regular 'gifts' of the Spirit (1 Cor. 12:10).

So the differences between Luke and Paul can be exaggerated, to the detriment of a balanced and comprehensive biblical understanding. Neither would confine their understanding of 'power for service' to the inside or the outside of the Church. To return to the question 'Why?' that heads this section, the twofold cord of salvation for self and service to others runs through both Acts and the Epistles. Baptism in Spirit brings purity and power.

At this point it will be helpful to summarise the chapter by putting the headings of sections and sub-sections together in a simple, easily remembered outline:

WHO?	Baptiser
	Believers
HOW?	Experience
	Evidence
WHEN?	Initiation
	Incorporation
WHY?	Salvation
	Service

With this chapter and chart we have reached the heart of this book. It is also a watershed. Everything so far has been building up to this and everything flows from it. It's downhill all the way from here. That does not mean there will be less to think about, but at least the chapters will be shorter! They will be easier to follow if the above outline has been memorised.

These eight features represent a comprehensive outline which covers everything the New Testament says about baptism in Spirit. The rest of this book concentrates on the Church rather than the Bible, sketching this aspect of her history from the end of the first century to the present, bringing it right up to date but with a longer perspective. To whet the reader's appetite, here is a 'trailer' of the whole story.

We shall trace the decline, over many centuries, in the understanding of Spirit baptism. One or other of the eight features was retained, but the whole eight-fold concept was lost. However, it began to be recovered from the seventeenth century onwards and looked like being fully recovered in the twentieth. Alas, now it looks as if this restoration is faltering. We need to ask why.

On a more positive note, we shall consider the efforts to achieve an integrated *theology* of Spirit baptism, without which it is unlikely to have a lasting and secure hold. Then we shall have to face the considerable problems of applying this *in practice* to the churches of today.

We end with a plea for the reconciliation of the deep differences between sacramental, evangelical and pentecostal streams on this issue, on the grounds that none is wholly right but all are partly right (and partly wrong). One can only try and imagine the effect of all three streams unitedly proclaiming to a divided and despairing world: 'Jesus will baptise you in one holy Spirit.'

5

The Traditional Teaching

How have the eight biblical features of baptism in Spirit fared during two millennia of church history? Have they been kept together? Have they been kept at all?

The whole era may be roughly (very roughly) divided into five periods:

(i) First to fifth centuries, during which baptism in Spirit persisted, more or less, in its original form, but tended to decline in importance.

(ii) Sixth to sixteenth centuries, during which the experiential dimension (the 'How?') was lost, significantly accompanied by the absence of 'baptismal' terminology. Ritual acts took its place.

(iii) Seventeenth to nineteenth centuries, during which the terminology was recovered, as was the experiential dimension, but the initiatory nature was lost and it became a 'second' work of grace (so the 'When?' got confused).

(iv) Twentieth century, during which it has been more talked about and experienced than at any previous time, with the rise of 'pentecostalism', but lacking any connection with salvation (half the 'Why?' was missing).

(v) The approach of the twenty-first century has seen a sudden and sharp decline in the baptismal dimension (the 'Who?') within both the older and newer churches who had begun to embrace it, tending to lead to the disappearance of the other dimensions as well, except in the pentecostal denominations, though even some of them are not as sure as they need to be.

To trace this development in detail would be far too much for a study of this scope. In any case, such research has already been done (and I shall quote one or two published works as we go).

While observing the general chronological stages, it will save time and space to treat the subject topically, highlighting *what* changes took place, rather than exactly *when* they occurred. In any case, the picture is more complicated than we have sketched. The changes have never been total. Each of the phases has persisted in part of the Church to this very day, so that 'medieval' and 'modern' concepts can be found side by side in the contemporary scene. We are really charting the origins of the different views held in the Church today.

We can begin by noting the persistence of baptism in Spirit during the first few centuries. It lasted much longer than the period covered by the New Testament (largely the first century AD). It can be found beyond the formation of the New Testament 'canon' (that is, the final recognition of which of the many 'books' then circulating carried 'apostolic' content and should be regarded as authoritative 'scripture' for the Church, a consensus which was finally reached by AD 367, when Athanasius listed the twenty-seven books with which we are familiar). There is a widespread theory that such supernatural phenomena as baptism in and gifts of the Spirit became obsolete once the scriptures were complete, so they died out (the technical term for this is 'cessationism'). It was held by Augustine, although in his last years he changed his opinion after witnessing healings; but it was his earlier view that was picked up by both Protestants and Catholics.

There is certainly evidence for a decline, but not to extinction. The best published research known to me is by two Catholic scholars, Kilian McDonnell and George T. Montague (*Christian Initiation and Baptism in the Holy Spirit*, Liturgical Press, 1991). It contains a list of 'Church Fathers' or 'Doctors' who speak about Spirit baptism, including Tertullian in North Africa, Hilary in Gaul, Cyril in Jerusalem, Basil in Cappadocia, Gregory Nazianzus in Constantinople, Philoxenus at Mabbug, John the Solitary at Apamea, Joseph Hazzaya in what is now Iraq, John Chrysostom in Jerusalem and Severus in Antioch. It is an impressive roll, both in space and time, up to the beginning of the sixth century.

The authors even find another reference, centuries later, in Symeon, the 'New Theologian', who called Spirit baptism the 'second' experience. Others had referred to the 'second baptism' or even the 'third birth'! What is quite clear from the sources quoted is that it was understood as a definite and conscious experience with inspired speech as the outward evidence (the authors refer to this as 'prophetic charisms', which is as good a label as any). A close association with water baptism is also a characteristic feature, remembering that in those days the 'catechumens', as candidates were called, were given months of 'catechetical' instruction to prepare them for the annual baptismal service at Easter, no doubt encouraging an expectancy of receiving the Spirit.

However, all this material is not allowed to disguise the fact that there was a continuous decline of the experience at the same time. This is put down to official reaction to Montanism, an early 'pentecostal' outbreak, itself a reaction to the growing formalism and institutionalism of the Church but inclined to extreme and excess, the result of unjudged prophecies by two women. While this may have been a factor, there is a much more obvious cause (see below).

As baptism in Spirit faded, so did the gifts of the Spirit, gradually but not entirely. For the research into this, read *Charismatic Gifts in the Early Church* by Professor Ronald Kydd (Hendrickson, 1984). The two – baptism in Spirit and the gifts of the Spirit – always go together. Where Spirit baptism is not confidently preached and readily experienced, the gifts also tend to disappear.

We must move on. As already indicated, the approach will be more topical than chronological, while not unrelated to the historical development. We shall chart the disappearance of one major feature after another, concentrating on the first word in each couplet of our outline in the previous chapter (e.g. 'Experience' under 'How?', 'Initiation' under 'When?').

EXPERIENCE LOST

The first dimension to disappear was the experiential nature of baptism in Spirit, together with its evidential accompaniment. Its place was taken over by other things which became substitutes. It was still believed to be happening, but in a form of which there was no need for anyone to be consciously aware. It became an automatic and inevitable result of other actions.

There are two examples of this change. The first in time is what we will call the 'sacramental', largely but not exclusively characteristic of the Roman Catholic Church. Later came what we will call the 'evangelical', resulting from the Protestant Reformation. There are both similarities and differences between the two.

Sacramental During those early centuries the Church became more institutionalised, especially after the Roman Emperor was converted and Christianity became the 'established' religion and even more so when the imperial power collapsed, leaving the Church to take its place (the bishop of Rome, later called 'Papa' or 'Pope', took over the imperial dress and titles!).

Worship became more formal. Ministry became more professional, dividing the Church into 'clergy' and 'laity', and more hierarchical, with the more charismatic apostles and prophets replaced by archbishops and bishops. Above all, this new 'priesthood' claimed a monopoly of dispensing the sacraments (we call this 'sacerdotalism'), which mediated the grace of God to the people. It was perhaps inevitable that baptism in Spirit became identified with these sacramental ministrations, eventually being replaced by them. We will look at three of these.

Christening The major reason for the loss of the experiential dimension was, I believe, the transfer of water baptism from adult catechumens, given through instruction beforehand, to babies, who could not be given any preparation at all. The inevitable result was a huge separation in time between water and Spirit baptism, destroying their New Testament association. I have gone into the reasons for this radical shift elsewhere (one was the teaching of Augustine that baptism dealt with inherited 'original' sin rather than committed 'actual' sins, thus saving babies from hell), but these do not directly concern us here. The effect of the change is relevant.

To cut a long story short, the ultimate result was to transfer baptism in Spirit to babies, too! But this meant leaving the experience and the evidence behind, since neither happened to babies. Put simply, it came to be believed and taught that babies were baptised in Spirit at the same time as they were baptised in water, but minus the trimmings, as it were. It was a short step to complete identification of the two baptisms as one and the same thing.

This is the view held by most Catholics today, including most of those who regard themselves as charismatics. Some (like Kilian McDonnell, already mentioned) claim babies receive the 'sensation' of Spirit baptism, but don't 'sense' it until much later, which is not a very convincing distinction.

For all practical purposes, water baptism, particularly when applied to babies, has replaced Spirit baptism, in spite of the New Testament evidence that they are neither simultaneous nor synonymous.

Chrismation This less common practice was also first applied to adults, then later transferred, with water baptism, to babies. It is simply an anointing with oil, usually on the head (a *chrism*, from which both 'Christ' and 'Christian' are derived). This was done occasionally before but commonly after water baptism, as a symbol of the Holy Spirit (as it is in scripture) – but was also considered to be a sacramental channel by means of which the Spirit would be imparted.

There is, of course, no scripture to support the need for anointing with oil to receive the Spirit (though it is there in connection with healing; Jas. 5:14-15). Yet only a few days before writing these lines I had a letter from a businessman who had just received the Spirit in precisely this manner (the only intelligible words in the torrent of language pouring from his mouth had been a repeated: 'Thank you, Lord'). I am not, however, advocating its use. I only mention this to illustrate the reason why it was originally introduced.

As with christening, chrismation lost its experiential expectation when, if not before, it was applied to babies. The outward act was believed adequate, without anything else happening. Once again, a sacramental act had become a substitute.

Confirmation This has become far more common. The custom is based on the biblical connection between the laying on of hands and baptism in Spirit, and taken further, on the basis on Acts 8, that it is an 'apostolic' prerogative (in spite of Ananias doing it in Acts 9!) and must now only be done by 'bishops' in the 'apostolic succession', a physical link with the original apostles through an imagined sequence of hands laid on from one generation to another (the 'Decretals' claiming this continuity are now known to be a forgery).

The transfer of baptism to babies made necessary the introduction of a ceremony for adult confirmation, as a supplementary recognition of the conscious acceptance of what had been done without the person's consent (there is no trace of this need in scripture, though there is the laying on of hands after baptism, usually immediately). Confirmation used to be quite secondary to baptism – bishops did the baptising and the local priest did the confirming. The practice and therefore the importance has been reversed almost universally.

Again, the act has replaced the experience, even though it is applied to adults! The wording of the confirmation liturgy reveals the biblical anticipation that the Spirit will be given through the laying on of hands; despite this, very few expect anything to happen at a confirmation service, though I know that many hope to 'feel something' at the time or to 'be different' afterwards, hopes which usually fade rapidly. However, I do know of one bishop who made a point of personally meeting every candidate *before* he confirmed them, to make sure he or she was already a penitent believer and to tell them the whole truth about baptism in Spirit so that they would expect to 'receive'. The congregations were astonished to 'see and hear' the results! Would that all bishops did the same. I would be 'almost persuaded' to join him in the Anglican denomination. I said 'almost'! I'd want to see water baptism brought back into close association with such Spirit baptisms (as it is in many cases, with the general decline in christening babies and the increase in adult conversions).

In all these three cases a sacramental act without an experiential or evidential content has become a substitute for baptism in Spirit. Not surprisingly, the terminology has also disappeared. The New Testament synonyms ('fall upon', 'plunged in', 'poured out', etc.) become unreal and inappropriate. The question, 'Have you received the Spirit?' is replaced by 'Have you been christened?' or 'Have you been confirmed?' We've come a long way from the apostles!

Evangelical The Protestant Reformers and their successors took a very different line. Their teaching had two primary emphases.

On the one hand, they were Christ-centred, focusing

on the second person of the Trinity to the relative neglect of the third. For example, Calvin's greatest work, his *Institutes of the Christian Religion*, has less than twenty pages about the Holy Spirit (but two hundred on the ten commandments, making his 'Calvinist' followers peculiarly vulnerable to legalism, of which the traditional Scottish sabbath is but one example).

On the other hand, they were faith-centred, focusing on the rediscovered doctrine of 'justification by faith', to which Luther, following Pelagius, added the word 'alone', which causes considerable confusion. Actually, scripture only once uses the word 'alone' in connection with justification by faith and then to state the exact opposite of Luther's intention – 'You see that a person is justified by what he does and not by faith alone' (Jas. 2:24). Little wonder that Luther called James' letter 'an epistle of straw' and advocated its removal from the New Testament!

This strong emphasis on 'faith alone' was bound to raise questions about sacraments, particularly infant baptism. Luther at first called it 'unbelievers' baptism', then said the faith of the Church made it effective, but finished up by challenging anyone to prove a baby didn't have faith!

But 'faith in Christ alone' would also have an effect on baptism in Spirit, coupled with a comparative dearth of teaching on the Holy Spirit. In fact, 'pentecostal terminology', as we have called the New Testament language, is conspicuous by its absence in the writings of the Reformers. Jesus is nowhere called the baptiser in Spirit and believers are nowhere said to be baptised in Spirit.

Christian initiation is described theologically as 'regeneration', the new birth. This was certainly said to be the work of the Holy Spirit. 'Born of the Spirit' (John 3:6,8), was commonly quoted. 'Baptised in the Spirit' was not.

Conversion became the evangelical substitute for Spirit baptism, though most evangelicals would not put it this way. They would want to say: 'Conversion *is* baptism in Spirit.' In making this equation, they necessarily cut out both experience and evidence from their definition.

Believing in Jesus and receiving the Spirit are run together into a widely used phrase in evangelical evangelism: 'receiving Jesus'. Whereas the sacramental approach regards baptism in water as the same as baptism in Spirit, the evangelical approach regards belief in Jesus as the same as baptism in Spirit.

The effect is the same in both approaches. Jesus is no longer preached as baptiser in Spirit and believers are no longer described as being baptised in Spirit. The 'pentecostal terminology' ('fall upon', 'plunged in', 'poured out', etc.) again becomes so inappropriate in the absence of any discernible experience that it drops out of use altogether.

'Born again' becomes the favourite description of Christian initiation, though it is found only five times in the New Testament and then only 'privately' within the Church (the conversation with Nicodemus, the Jewish theologian, is the only exception). By contrast, 'baptised in Spirit' is found seven times and could hardly have been used more 'publicly'.

If challenged about this non-use, evangelicals will say they believe in 'baptism in Spirit' as an equivalent term for 'conversion', but still won't use it in their preaching, especially now that it has been given a different connotation in the 'pentecostal' stream. However, if they believe the latter is mistaken, they should surely correct this by using the 'pentecostal terminology' of scripture with what they consider the proper meaning, rather than neglecting it altogether. The silence suggests they are actually embarrassed by such language, presumably because of its associations in the book of Acts, which never mentions 'regeneration' or being 'born again', but concentrates on the two (distinct) aspects of initiation – believing in Jesus and receiving the Spirit.

With the absence of Spirit baptism from their thinking came an inevitable neglect of the supernatural gifts of the Spirit. Following Augustine and the Reformers, most evangelicals have been 'cessationists', who believe such extraordinary abilities ceased long ago, with either the death of the apostles or the completion of the New Testament scriptures. Only recently has this attitude changed.

In passing, it may be remarked that an excessive emphasis on 'faith alone' also has a detrimental effect on the understanding of repentance. At most, evangelicals allow this to be expressed in *words* (a brief repeated 'sinner's prayer') but seem reluctant to insist on 'proving repentance by *deeds*' (as Paul did, following John the baptiser's example; Luke 3:8; Acts 26:20). That, for an evangelical, comes dangerously close to combining works with faith.

It is time to leave this loss of the experiential dimension of Spirit baptism, both in the sacramental and evangelical streams, which was for considerable periods universal in the Church. This situation has changed in the last few centuries.

INITIATION LOST

From the seventeenth to the nineteenth centuries the language of baptism in Spirit gradually returned to Christian pulpits. Significantly, this was because it began again to be understood as a distinct experience, different from repenting, believing or being baptised in water.

However, there was a 'downside' to this recovery. Baptism in Spirit was disconnected from initiation and over this period became more and more a 'subsequent' or 'second' stage, associated with sanctification rather than justification. We shall sketch this development by looking at two groups.

Puritan It is to the Puritans of the seventeenth century that we probably owe the rediscovery of 'baptism in Spirit'.

There is no point in my going into much detail when this is already available in print. I refer to the excellent researches of Michael Eaton and his M.Th thesis for the University of South Africa, now published as *Baptism with the Spirit, the Teaching of Martyn Lloyd-Jones* (Inter-Varsity Press, 1989). He considers the late minister of Westminster Chapel in London to be the best modern exponent of the Puritan understanding, but the value of his book for our purpose is that he thoroughly examines the views of the earlier Puritans as well, even beginning as far back as John Calvin, regarded as a spiritual father by most of them. And he takes the story as far forward as Jonathan Edwards, the revivalist in New England. In between, he considers Richard Sibbes, Thomas Goodwin and John Owen.

Our interest is in the meaning and significance given to baptism in Spirit by these men. The author's preference for 'with' rather than 'in' and the tendency to avoid calling Jesus the baptiser may or may not be significant. We can summarise the Puritan understanding as follows:

(i) It is a *definite* experience. It may even be considered an 'overwhelming' experience, in which the recipient is flooded (liquid language is readily used) with a sense of the divine presence around and within.

(ii) It is a *subsequent* experience. It is quite distinct from regeneration, though some might add that it could conceivably occur at the same time or at least soon after. But a person can and must be fully regenerate before it can happen.

(iii) It is a *confirming* experience. Its main function is to give a high degree of assurance to the regenerate.

For this reason, Puritans frequently referred to it as a 'seal', the divine stamp on those he has justified.

(iv) It is a *self-evident* experience. However, at this point, the Puritans tended to diverge from the 'evidence' associated with Spirit baptism in scripture. They emphasised the fruit rather than any prophetic gifting: in particular, exuberance and confidence. However, both would help witnessing to be more effective, though they tended to see this done from a pulpit, where they looked for preaching that was 'anointed', that had 'unction'.

Dr Lloyd Jones' own book on the subject was significantly entitled *Joy Unspeakable* (Kingsway, 1984). Many of his followers were shocked that he drew such a sharp distinction between conversion and baptism in Spirit; his memorable response was: 'Got it all at conversion? Then where is it all?' His background in the Welsh revival coloured his understanding, as did his Calvinistic emphasis on the sovereignty of God. So far as I know, he was not in the practice of laying on hands for the reception of baptism.

The Puritans tended to be cessationist in regard to the gifts of the Spirit, and so reinterpreted them in a more 'ordinary' way. Prophecy was seen as 'anointed' preaching (but they kept it to men; cf. 1 Cor. 11:5 with 1 Tim. 2:12). Healing was limited to praying for the sick. 'Tongues' was the ability to learn a foreign language quickly in order to serve on the mission field.

To sum up, the Puritans recovered some, though not

all, of the eight biblical dimensions we listed in Chapter 4. They spoke freely of baptism in Spirit for believers but were slow to call Jesus the baptiser. They saw it as an experience, but did not pick up the same 'prophetic' evidence (theirs was internal rather than external). They severed it from initiation and incorporation (1 Corinthians 12:13 was taken to refer to regeneration, not Spirit baptism). They saw it as directly assisting service, but were unsure about its link with salvation, other than confirming justification and motivating evangelism.

The big plus was that baptism in Spirit was back on the agenda. But it was to take a rather strange turn in the eighteenth and nineteenth centuries.

Holiness The Evangelical Revival of the eighteenth century was to set the course for this change. The first major figure, the Calvinist George Whitefield, stayed with the Puritan understanding of baptism in Spirit as the assurance of justification. The Arminians John and Charles Wesley, who took over when Whitefield left for America, were to link it to sanctification, though neither actually spoke about 'baptism in Spirit' except in very general and rather vague terms.

This is what happened. The Wesley brothers sought sanctification before they knew justification. While students at Oxford, where Whitefield was a college servant, they and he started what they called 'The Holy Club'; others nicknamed them 'Methodists' because of their disciplined devotions, allocation of time and social welfare. It was only after their failure as missionaries in the New World that John and Charles came into a real knowledge of 'sins forgiven and hope of heaven' in May 1738. At an all-night prayer meeting the following January, the Spirit 'fell on' them in a memorable way.

Their father's dying words were, 'The inward witness, son. That is the proof, the strongest proof, of Christianity.' John's sermons and Charles's hymns are full of assurance, with a strong emphasis on the Holy Spirit. But the brothers never lost their quest for sanctification. John believed that God raised up Methodism 'to spread scriptural holiness throughout the land'. He was not content (as Whitefield had tended to be) to see thousands converted. He organised them into districts, circuits, societies, classes and bands in order that they could encourage each other into holy living.

But he developed a distinctive doctrine of sanctific-ation, which encouraged the expectation of a second 'crisis experience' in the Christian life (the first being conversion), which would deliver from all known sin and fill the heart with 'perfect love', leaving no room for self or sin. Thus, the two-stage concept of salvation took root, with two peak experiences, one of justification and the other of sanctification. This 'scheme' was to have profound repercussions, right up to the present.

While Wesley saw this 'Christian perfection', as he boldly called it, as being 'full of the Holy Spirit', he did not call the second stage 'baptism in the Holy Spirit'. That was left to one of his colleagues, a French Swiss, Flêcher of Nyon on the shores of Lake Geneva (I have had the privilege of preaching to crowded congregations in his church there; so famous was he that the street on which it stands is named Rue de Flêcher). After he moved to Cheshire as a vicar, he was known as 'Fletcher of Madeley' and gained the reputation of being 'the saintliest man in all of England'. Wesley chose him to be his successor as the leader of Methodism, but he predeceased him. Fletcher was the very first to label the second blessing of 'entire sanctification' as 'baptism in the Spirit'. Little did he realise what he had done!

To hurry the story along, this two-stage salvation, with the second identified with Spirit baptism, crossed the Atlantic and spawned a variety of what came to be known as 'Holiness movements', which inevitably became denominations, some of which have now re-crossed the same ocean and crossed others.

One of the best-known exponents of this view was the evangelist and teacher Charles Finney who stamped it deeply into the American soul. He, too, like Wesley, became dissatisfied with simply getting many converted. Towards the end of his life, he concentrated on propagating Spirit baptism as the experience of 'entire sanctification'. As someone has put it, the language of Pentecost was now joined to the language of Calvary in his preaching (see *The Promise of the Spirit* by Charles G. Finney, a collection of his last lectures and letters, Bethany, 1980).

Holiness 'camp meetings' in the United States urged many to seek baptism in Spirit. Finney came to Britain, in the wake of D.L. Moody's evangelistic crusades, to press it on the many new converts. A book by William

Boardman, a Presbyterian (significantly entitled *The Higher Christian Life*) motivated a couple, Pearsall and Hannah Whitall Smith, to hold camp meetings, first in Oxford and Brighton and then in the Lake District, where the camp meeting later became the Keswick Convention; today this has offshoots around the world (though its teaching is now considerably different from the early years, baptism in Spirit having been moved from sanctification back to justification, the classic evangelical position).

We have already stated that there is little basis in scripture for baptism in Spirit being the introduction of a state of 'entire sanctification'. The Epistles of the New Testament, as we said, are addressed to those who have already been baptised in Spirit but who can hardly be described as 'entirely sanctified'! Yet this mistaken notion in Holiness circles was rendering a significant service to the Church at large, explaining its penetration into many older denominations. It was a healthy and much needed reminder that sanctification is as much part of salvation as justification, and that the Lord has made adequate provision for both, which are alike appropriated by faith. Holiness is not only demanded of God's people; it is offered to them as a work of grace.

Those are the pluses; but there were minuses. Sanctification was seen as an instantaneous acquisition. Baptism in Spirit was fixed as a 'second' or 'subsequent' event, dissociated from initiation. The proof of its happening was seen in later fruit rather than in immediate gift (especially the 'prophetic'). It was primarily concerned with salvation for self rather than service to others. It was not yet the full New Testament concept. These deficiencies would lead to a reaction in the next century.

It was largely though not exclusively out of this Holiness movement that twentieth-century pentecostalism was to emerge, which makes it so significant for our story.

SALVATION LOST

The title to this section must not be misunderstood. I am not referring to the issue of whether a believer can lose their salvation or not (for this, see my *Once Saved, Always Saved?*, Hodder and Stoughton, 1996). I am referring to the fact that the most notable development in the last hundred years is that baptism in Spirit has lost its connection with salvation, either justification or sanctification. We must now follow the course of this major shift.

Pentecostal The rise of 'pentecostalism' may be traced back to the very first day (and night) of the twentieth century, January 1st 1901. Students at a Bible college in Topeka, Kansas, spent all night in prayer, asking the Lord Jesus to baptise them in his Spirit. But there was a difference, a new content to their prayer. They were seeking the same experience and therefore the same evidence (particularly 'tongues') as they had learned happened at Pentecost. True to Jesus' promise to those who 'go on asking', they received.

Almost simultaneously, there was a similar happening at a 'black and white' mission hall in Azusa Street in Los Angeles, which soon spread across the States and around the world, reaching Sunderland, England, via Norway.

Alas, it was rejected when it began to penetrate older churches, often contemptuously dismissed as 'the tongues movement', though this was only one of the spiritual gifts that reappeared (it may have been the most frequent or the most unusual, thus drawing more attention). Prophecy and healing were the most prominent of the others.

The major reasons for this rejection were probably more social and cultural than theological. 'Pentecostalism' reached the lower working classes, whereas the established churches tended to cater for the middle and upper classes. Worship tended to equate noise with power and was much less inhibited and more participatory. It was 'just too much' for respectable religious tradition.

The result was the founding of a multiplicity of new churches and denominations during the first half of the twentieth century, many of them black. They were regarded with suspicion and sometimes actively opposed and persecuted by existing branches of Christendom. They preached and practised 'the baptism of the Spirit', though in most other areas of doctrine they were orthodox evangelicals, strongly influenced by the 'dispensational' teaching of J. Nelson Darby, founder of the Brethren, probably mediated to them through the Scofield Bible. This lay behind their vivid expectancy of the imminent return of the Lord Jesus.

So how did they understand Spirit baptism? Though

there were some variations among them, we may list the things they held in common.

First, it was a *second* crisis experience, after being 'born again'. This was inherited from the Holiness movement and has remained an unquestioned (and unquestionable!) constant in their beliefs ever since. It has nothing to do with becoming a Christian, but comes later, often much later. This doctrine of 'subsequence', as it is called, is one of the major stumbling blocks to full integration with other churches.

Second, *tongues* are regarded as 'the initial evidence', the one and only proof that someone has received 'the baptism of the Spirit', as they invariably call it. There are few exceptions to their absolute insistence on this (the Elim denomination in Britain is one). This is the other stumbling block to other Christians, seeming to them to go beyond biblical warrant.

Third, it is power for *service*, not salvation. This was the most radical change from the Holiness movement and the main reason for the separate development of the pentecostal movement. They were right to avoid the notion of Spirit baptism as 'entire sanctification' but wrong to sever all connection with sanctification – or justification or glorification, for that matter. As the older teaching had gone beyond scripture, the new view wouldn't even go as far as scripture.

Perhaps the greatest difficulty this understanding faces when tested by scripture is the fact we have already exposed and emphasised – that in the New Testament, being 'baptised in' the Spirit and 'receiving' the Spirit are one and the same thing, thus tying it to initiation and to salvation. Pentecostals simply ignore – or avoid when faced with – the implications of this equation. They postulate *two* receptions of the Spirit by the believer, one without experience or evidence at the beginning (for salvation) and the other with both coming later (for service), one for purity and the other for power. We have already questioned whether such a division can be found in the New Testament.

But five of the eight dimensions had been recovered. And pentecostalism was clearly meeting a need, as its rapid growth indicated. The churches that resulted were in many respects much more akin to the New Testament churches in atmosphere and clientele. When the young Prince Charles was on 'walkabout' in Australia, he was taken to an aboriginal 'pentecostal' mission one Sunday and wrote home to his mother, Queen Elizabeth the Second: 'If this is what early Christianity was like, I can understand how it spread.' Bishop Lesslie Newbigin, of the Church of South India, was one of the first to recognise pentecostalism as the 'third force' in Christendom, alongside the Catholic and evangelical streams, in a remarkably prophetic book, *The Household of God* (S.C.M., 1953). It could only be a matter of time before this distinctive contribution infiltrated the other two streams. It began to happen in the 1960s.

Neo-pentecostal A number of different factors contributed to the appearance of 'neo-' (i.e. new) pentecostals within the older denominations. A single book (*The Cross and the Switchblade*), written by a young Pentecostal pastor, David Wilkerson, working in downtown USA among street-gang kids, had an influence out of all proportion, speaking strongly to the emerging youth culture. An Armenian dairy farmer in America founded the Full Gospel Business Men's Fellowship Incorporated (another example of the Spirit loosening the tongue!), which spread baptism in Spirit among laymen the world over.

But the clergy were not far behind. In the States, Dennis Bennett, an ex-Methodist Episcopalian (and his famous book, *Nine O' Clock in the Morning*) and Larry Christenson of the Lutherans, soon with many others, were opening up their denominations to pentecostal experience. In Britain, Michael Harper founded the Fountain Trust to spread it. In 1967, baptism and gifts of the Spirit burst on the Roman Catholic scene, to the surprise of many and the consternation of most pentecostals; one of the few brave exceptions was the South African, David du Plessis, who headed off for Rome itself, where Pope John XXIII had been praying for 'a new Pentecost'. Those were heady days for those of us who shared in them.

But the purpose of this book is not primarily historical. It is to see how far these developments recovered the full New Testament understanding and experience.

At first, the pentecostal doctrine was taken into main-line denominations with the experience. The approach was pragmatic. If their teaching restored the power so lacking in other parts of the Church, then it must be all right. There was very little difference between traditional, or as it was later called 'classical' pentecostal, and neo-pentecostal preaching and publishing. Terminology was much the same, so the theology was also much the same; the two are closely linked.

There was, however, one real difference in practice. Whereas pentecostals saw the 'power for service' to be used in evangelism outside the church, neo-pentecostals tended to concentrate on edification inside the church. They not only faced the task of 'converting' their fellow members to this new experience; they had seen, perhaps more clearly, its relevance to the body of Christ. So there was more talk about 'gifts for the body', which began to break down the ritualism of worship, the formalism of fellowship and the clericalism of ministry.

However, it was not long before it was realised that all this would not last without a solid foundation of biblical theology underneath it. 'Classic' pentecostals have tended, until recently, to be suspicious of theology, on the grounds that empowerment is more fruitful than enlightenment. But churches with longer experience understand that both are necessary. Heat and light are a highly combustible combination! Spirit and Word need each other.

So theologians began to work on this new dimension and quickly discovered the shortcomings of pentecostal doctrine when carefully examined in the light of scripture, particularly in the aspects of 'evidence' and 'subsequence', neither of which seemed justified by the biblical data as a whole.

This left a theological vacuum, which a number tried to fill. We shall consider their efforts in Chapter 6, but will move on with our survey here, to note what happened to baptism in Spirit over the last few decades of this century.

BAPTISM LOST

Gradually, and then more rapidly, talk about Jesus as baptiser or believers as baptised faded. The adjective 'pentecostal' was used less and less outside pentecostal denominations. It was replaced by:

Charismatic The pentecostal infiltration into the main-line churches gave way to 'the charismatic renewal'. This change of label was profoundly significant. It is derived from the Greek word *charismata*, used of the 'spiritual gifts' in 1 Corinthians 12-14. It diverts attention away from baptism in Spirit to the gifts of the Spirit.

This exactly reflects what was happening in reality. The gifts were increasingly accepted, but the baptism was increasingly rejected. One was widely wanted; the other was not. The exercise of gifts was more acceptable than the experience of baptism.

This trend was accelerated by two men; one travelled the world and the other left that to his books. Both were associated with Fuller Seminary in California – John Wimber and Peter Wagner. Neither had had an experience comparable with what pentecostals called 'the baptism' but both wanted to see supernatural 'power', in the form of extraordinary abilities, fully restored to the Church, primarily for the purpose of mission.

They were more comfortable with the Gospels than Acts, taking the pre-Pentecost ministry of Jesus and his disciples as a model. There was much talk about healing diseases and casting out demons, little about the day of Pentecost and even less about the gift of tongues.

Their declared objective was to restore the power of the Holy Spirit to the whole evangelical constituency by encouraging the gifts of the Spirit without 'the baptism', which had been the main stumbling-block for them. There could surely be no real objection to the gifts, since they were clearly taught in scripture and evangelicals prided themselves on being scriptural, in belief and behaviour. In other words, they set about removing 'cessationism' without introducing 'pentecostalism'.

They coined a new phrase for what they believed was a new phase in the Holy Spirit's work in the twentieth century, namely 'Third Wave'. The 'first wave' had been the growth of pentecostalism outside the churches during the first half of the century. The 'second wave' had seen the same thing happening inside the older churches but only as a sizeable minority. This new 'third wave' would spread the rediscovered power of the Spirit throughout the churches, and particularly through the healthier evangelical parts, by removing the peculiar and offensive 'baptism in the Spirit' from the package.

Few were aware of this deletion at the time. They were too distracted by the good things that were happening, the 'signs and Wimbers', as one wag wittily labelled them. But it represented a radical reversal in 'the renewal': even 'charismatic' was on the way out.

It left a vacuum in spiritual experience, which had been filled by 'being baptised in the Holy Spirit' since the turn of the century. Human nature, like nature, abhors a vacuum. What would step into its place?

Contemporary   We cannot give a label to this final section because quite a number of things have come into the gap – and gone again, usually after quite a short spell of about two years. But they have one thing in common. They have each helped to change the word 'renewal' for another: 'revival'.

There had been some groups on the fringe of the pentecostal movement which were based on the belief that the 'end-times' had come and with them, therefore, the last generations, or even generation, to live on the earth before Jesus returned. It was the time for the Church to reach its peak of quality, and perhaps quantity, as the 'pure bride' of Christ or the 'manifest sons of God', as some of them were called.

At the same time, other groups were becoming more 'post-millennial' (the belief that Jesus would return after the Church had first set up his kingdom on earth by taking over the government of the nations). There was talk of 'restoration' and 'reconstruction'. The atmosphere was 'triumphalist', anticipating a universal take-over by a revitalised Church.

This mixture of high ideals and hopes had been filtering

into the charismatic renewal over some years, particularly through the rash of new churches it had produced and some of the transatlantic links that had been formed. Many transferred from older churches to be part of what was coming.

The common denominator was the conviction that it was high time for 'revival' on a scale surpassing all previous revivals. It was time for the 'latter rains' to fall, prior to the ushering in of the kingdom of God.

Every fresh outbreak of the activity of the Spirit was eagerly welcomed as a possible harbinger of the big one, world-wide revival, and none more so than the spectacular happenings at the then newly-formed Airport Church in Toronto, Canada. Some extraordinary phenomena, not seen on such a scale since the ministry of Jonathan Edwards in New England, were drawing dried-up pastors and their thirsty members by the thousand from all over the world. The involuntary physical occurrences were attracting the most attention, but many were being 'blessed'.

Visitors returning to their own countries carried the happenings back with them, above all the English. Staid Anglican churches were revolutionised, some of their members scandalised!

But what to make of it? Some labelled it the 'fourth wave', the final move of the Spirit in the century before the new millennium arrived. Others believed the big 'IT', the world-wide revival, had now begun.

One of the major questions that arose was how it related to scripture. Many felt it was not necessary to ask this. Surely the Spirit was totally free to act in unprecedented and 'unbiblical' ways? Others felt that without scriptural warrant there was no objective criterion for deciding what was of the Spirit and what wasn't, since there is usually a mixture of God, man and Satan during times of spiritual excitement. For example, was it right to refer to all the emotional and physical accompaniments as 'manifestations', a biblical word for the workings of the Spirit? Was this an example of the 'times [seasons] of refreshing' foretold by Peter (Acts 3:19)? Above all, was this a fulfilment of the promise that 'he will baptise you in holy Spirit' or was it more a 'blessing' from God?

I, along with many others, dared to write a book in which I tackled this very issue (*Is the Blessing Biblical?*, Hodder and Stoughton, 1995). In the light of scripture, I had come to the conclusion that the phenomena (weeping and laughing, falling and jumping, even animal noises) were human reactions rather than divine actions, but that they could be the result of a genuine encounter with the Lord – though not necessarily, especially where there was a high degree of expectancy or of human suggestion or manipulation. I could not regard them as evidence for baptism in Spirit in the absence of any 'prophetic charisms'. In fact, only one of the eight features of baptism in Spirit was left – experience!

There was as much, if not more, appeal to tradition rather than scripture, for precedents to validate what was happening. John Wesley and Jonathan Edwards were quoted more widely than any of the Apostles. Later church history seemed to carry more weight than the book of Acts. It is hard to maintain experience without an undergirding of clear biblical theology. Not surprisingly, the 'Toronto blessing' (note the need for new language when biblical terminology doesn't clearly fit) has already begun to decline, leaving some churches no longer growing; some have even shrunk.

What will be the next 'wave'? Delving into church history for ideal models has persisted but is now pushing further back, beyond the 'revivals' of the last three centuries. As I write, the current quest is for Celtic Christianity, that earlier version resulting from the work of Patrick in Ireland, Columba in Scotland on the Isle of Iona, Aidan and Cuthbert in England on the 'Holy Island' of Lindisfarne in Northumbria – before it was swamped at the Synod of Whitby in 663 by Catholic Christianity, introduced to England via Canterbury by the other Augustine sent by Pope Gregory.

What we really need to do is to go right back to what has been called 'primitive Christianity', but which I prefer to call 'apostolic Christianity', as described in the book of Acts and the Epistles addressed to the same churches. If we really believe that the Bible is the final authority on all matters of belief and behaviour, we must be willing to engage in biblical study. 'Do your best to present yourself to God as one approved, a workman who does not need to be ashamed and who correctly handles the word of truth' (2 Tim. 2:15).

Before leaving this chapter, it will be helpful to bring it all together by looking at all the changes in a single chart (see below, pp. 216-7). We can then see at a glance how true – or not true – each view has been to the full New Testament understanding of baptism in Spirit.

Down the left-hand side are listed the eight major distinctives we noted in Chapter 4, under the four basic questions. Along the top are the eight different views we have covered in this chapter, under the four basic deletions. The two are correlated in the columns.

We can now make some observations on the total picture revealed in the chart.

(i)   None of the different positions has managed to hold all eight features together!

(ii) The profound difference between the sacramental and evangelical positions on the one hand and the pentecostal on the other becomes very clear and indicates how much both will need to change to unite.

(iii) Yet they are complementary. Sacramentals and evangelicals have concentrated on 'when' and 'why', pentecostals on 'who' and 'how'. Both seem right in what they affirm and wrong in what they deny!

(iv) Only the 'first wave' of pentecostalism clearly preached Christ the 'baptiser'.

(v)   'Baptism in Spirit' terminology is not used where it is not thought of as a definite experience (more of this in Chapter 6). It re-emerged from the seventeenth century on, reaching a peak in the twentieth, but is now in serious decline.

(vi) Its reappearance tended to be as a 'second' or

'subsequent' event to conversion and has remained that way.

The decline and possible disappearance of baptism in Spirit from churches other than pentecostal (and even now among some of them!) has a serious consequence. In spite of 'third wave' hopes, many have observed that where *baptism* in the Spirit is neither confidently preached nor consciously experienced, the supernatural *gifts* of the Spirit also decline and eventually disappear. This happened in the early Church and has now begun to happen again.

Let a South African bear witness to this: Michael Cassidy (in his book *Bursting the Wineskins*, Hodder and Stoughton, 1983) quotes two of his (and my) friends. 'Perhaps only Michael Green does full justice to the astonishing evidence of the 20th-century charismatic renewal which has received its major impetus and perhaps its spiritual power and effectiveness from the sustained preaching of Baptism in the Spirit.' He also quotes Derek Crumpton, pioneer of the renewal in that country: 'Evangelicals may argue about the terminology. But the evidence is that where this teaching (i.e. Baptism of the Spirit as a clear experience) is given, the resultant response is undeniable ... I have also observed that wherever this emphasis is lacking, the renewing move of the Spirit loses impact, momentum and meaning.' Those who are puzzled by the apparent decease of the 'charismatic renewal' need look no further for a reason.

Those who believe that baptism in Spirit has a central

and fundamental place in the life of the individual believer and the corporate Church will be deeply concerned about this growing neglect and eager to do everything possible to restore it to its proper place.

However, I do not see that happening until there is a strong theological understanding that gives confidence to both pulpit and pew that this is indeed God's will for his people, at all times and in all places. But it will have to be a new theology that integrates the insights that are truly biblical from all the views we have reviewed.

In chapter 6 we shall ask whether such a theological integration is *possible*, looking at the necessary 'shape' of it. In Chapter 7 we shall ask whether it is *likely* to be accepted and applied. The answers will be neither optimistic nor pessimistic, but very realistic!

		EXPERIENCE LOST	
	Chapter 5	Sacramental	Evangelical
Chapter 4			
WHO?	Baptiser		
	Believers		
HOW?	Experience		
	Evidence		
WHEN?	Initiation	√	√
	Incorporation	√	√
WHY?	Salvation	√	√
	Service	?	?

| INITIATION LOST | | SALVATION LOST | | BAPTISM LOST | |
Puritan	Holiness	Pentecostal	Neo-Pentecostal	Charismatic	Contemporary
		1st Wave	2nd Wave	3rd Wave	4th Wave
	?	√	?		
√	√	√	√		
√	√	√	√	?	√
?	?	√	√	?	?
				√	
				√	
√	√			?	?
?	?	√	√	√	?

6

The Recent Revisions

Both pentecostals and neo-pentecostals tended to be pragmatic, more concerned with spreading an experience of baptism in Spirit than with an understanding of it, particularly a *theological* understanding.

But the far-seeing began to realise that the experience could not be commended or communicated to the whole Church unless it could be supported by a sound biblical exegesis. There was also a need to integrate this with the theology already held in the churches. The basic issue was whether this 'new' doctrine (new only to the churches today but as 'old' as the early Church) could be contained within the existing credal formulations or whether it would be a case of new wine bursting the old wineskins.

A veritable battalion of theologians has tackled this question, but I am not going to duplicate the work that has already been done in collecting the fruits of their labour. The best book I know to cover this is *Treasures Old and New – interpretations of 'Spirit baptism' in the charismatic renewal movement*, a doctoral dissertation for the University of South Africa by Henry I. Lederle (Hendricksen, 1988). While I shall have reason to criticise his personal conclusion, I heartily recommend this comprehensive compendium to those who want to study the subject in depth (and breadth). He covers a great number of names – Dennis Bennett, Larry Christenson, Stephen Clark, Peter Hocken, Rodman Williams and Howard Ervin (for the 'neo-pentecostal' interpretation); Cardinal Suenens, Kilian McDonnell, Kevin Ranaghan, Simon Tugwell, Eusebius Stephanou and John Gunstone (for the 'sacramental' interpretation); Tom Smail, David Watson, Michael Harper, Michael Cassidy, Arnold Bittlinger, Siegfried Grossmann, Francis Sullivan and Morton Kelsey (for what he calls the 'integrative' interpretation) and many others less well known. His analysis and mine are similar, but I want to subdivide this third group and combine the first and second.

Though they vary in detail, I find that all these attempts to integrate pentecostal experience into existing theology can be put into just two categories, those that leave that theology unchanged and those that require it to be changed (though the degree of adjustment may vary). This may seem simplistic but has the great advantage of going to the heart of the issue under debate, as well as highlighting the practical problems of application (which we explore in Chapter 7). For reasons which will soon be apparent, the two categories are labelled 'Delayed experience' and 'Definite event'.

DELAYED EXPERIENCE

The majority of attempts to integrate traditional theology and pentecostal experience have resorted to divorcing the experience from the baptism, allowing a time-gap between the two. In other words, the experience and its accompanying evidence are not an essential element to baptism in Spirit *at the time*. That can come later, much later or even not at all. Whenever – or even whether – it later becomes a conscious experience does not affect the fact that baptism in Spirit has taken place earlier, without conscious awareness.

Removing the experiential dimension as essential to the event leaves the field wide open for anyone to put it anywhere they choose in the *orda salutis*, the sequence of salvation. It is not surprising, therefore, that both 'sacramental' and 'evangelical' theologians have eagerly embraced this approach. One group is free to identify Spirit baptism with water baptism, usually of infants; the other identifies it with 'conversion'.

In both cases, there is no need to change the theology already held. 'Baptism in Spirit' is merely another label for what is already believed and practised. There is, however, an addition, if no change – namely, the possibility and even the desirability of a later conscious realisation of what has already happened. There are obvious benefits to someone becoming fully aware in practice of what they already possess in principle. A baby can inherit a fortune but may not have the pleasure of spending it until years later, to put the case in its simplest form. In the same way, someone who has been baptised in the Spirit (say, at christening or conversion) may not enjoy his presence for themselves or use his power for others until much later.

I call this 'time-bomb' theology! The bomb is secretly planted without anyone being aware of it until it is later detonated and explodes, when everyone nearby knows about it.

So what's wrong with it? It seems such a simple and obvious solution, enabling the whole Church to welcome pentecostal experience without having to adopt pentecostal doctrine (especially 'substance' and 'evidence'). Furthermore, it requires no reformation of traditional teaching and therefore no repentance for mistaken instruction.

Well, for one thing, it runs into a language problem. And terminology is vital to theology. What we say affects how we think, as well as vice versa.

Which do we call 'baptism in Spirit', the unconscious event or the later conscious experience?

Some, seeking to be consistent with the New Testament, have tried hard to apply the term to both, seeing event and experience as parts of one whole. But this is a difficult exercise in mental gymnastics, especially when they are separated by many years and one is not even able to be consciously remembered.

There is a parallel to the problem in connection with water baptism. The increasing demand to enjoy this as an experience by those already christened as babies led some Anglican and Presbyterian churches to offer a novel ceremony of 'confirmation by immersion', offering to dip them in water to 'complete' their baptism, or at least to make it a conscious memory. But which was their 'baptism', the earlier or the later occasion? The clerical administrator would probably plump for the former, to keep his theology and conscience intact! The lay recipient would almost certainly point to the latter if asked about their baptism. Few would find it easy to say it was both. That would mean they had only been 'half' baptised the first time and only 'fully' baptised the second, which cannot possibly be justified from the scriptures relating to water baptism.

Neither can a breakdown of Spirit baptism into separate events, separated in time. So a choice has to be made. Is the earlier unconscious event or the later conscious experience to be called 'baptism in Spirit'?

The synonyms for 'baptised' (e.g. 'fall upon', 'poured out upon'), to say nothing of the word itself, clearly speak of the Spirit coming from *outside* to a person, whereas the view we are considering sees the later experience as coming from the Spirit already *inside*. That would seem to rule out speaking of that as the 'baptism'.

So almost all 'time-bomb' theologians, whether sacramental or evangelical, choose to apply the term to the earlier unconscious event, thus dissociating it from what is described in the book of Acts as a conscious experience (the few exceptions, like Michael Eaton, are then accused of adopting the pentecostal doctrine of 'subsequence'). They often refer to the later experience as 'what pentecostals call "baptism in the Spirit"', with the clear implication that they themselves do not. So what do they call it? That depends – on whether they see the later awareness as a single or multiple experience.

Single Some see the need for a clear and definite moment of entry into a conscious enjoyment of the Spirit's presence and power. A whole range of words have been used to identify and communicate this, the most common being 'the *release* of the Spirit'. The clumsiest suggestion is 'actualisation'. Ugh!

Multiple Others see a string of conscious experiences, the first no different from the rest. They seem fond of the word 'filled' (which was used in scripture for the first and later experiences, Acts 2:4; 4:31, unlike all the other synonyms, which were used only of the first). I have even read, more than once, that we can expect many, many 'anointings' and even many 'baptisms', but at that point language begins to mean anything we want it to mean and we are about to join Alice in Wonderland.

So *in theory*, 'baptism in Spirit' language is not applied to any later experience, whether single or multiple, but is limited to the earlier event in this theology. Actually, *in practice*, the term is hardly used at all. Perhaps this is because it would invite unfavourable comparisons with how it is described in scripture.

In fact, this approach virtually returns to the traditional sacramental and evangelical positions in which Spirit baptism plays little or no part. Yet it has been widely welcomed. There are two simple reasons for its popularity.

First, it offers *least change*. The status quo is a very solid body to shift. Beliefs that have been held for centuries, or even decades, are not quickly relinquished. The Church has always been more ready to add new notions than to subtract old ones. It is obviously much easier to incorporate a new experience if it requires no rethink of well-established assumptions.

Second, it offers *less challenge*. It is much less disturbing to tell a congregation, 'You've already been baptised in Spirit and only need to become aware of it', than to say, 'You need to be baptised in Spirit if you haven't been already.' Paul's question ('Having believed, did you receive holy Spirit?' Acts 19:2) doesn't need to be asked or answered.

Nevertheless, it is a compromise, which always carries a cost. Four out of the eight features of New Testament baptism in Spirit have been lost, with the consequence that the other four tend to fade into insignificance as well. The ultimate result is to lose Spirit baptism altogether from the preaching of the gospel, concentrating on what Jesus *did* for us long ago rather than what he *does* for us now as the ascended Lord.

The practical result is that fewer and fewer people have a conscious relationship with the third Person of the Trinity. They know and talk freely about Father and Son, but not the Spirit. I have discovered that there are Christians in almost every church I visit who have this personal and intimate knowledge of the Spirit, but they usually got it in a church where baptism in Spirit was preached confidently as a conscious experience, not in a church of the 'time-bomb' outlook, where the teachers have the problem of what scriptures you can use to encourage the 'delayed experience', without calling it baptism in Spirit. So, in fact, not even that is 'ministered' to the people, either publicly or privately.

There are some variations within this group of theological schemes, most notably the different opinion as to whether baptism in Spirit happens at christening or conversion, but these are not significant enough to warrant separate examination. If the basic factor of separating out the experience is common to them all, as it is, we have said enough to show that this is not the way, either in theory or practice, to integrate the pentecostal experience into the rest of the Church.

DEFINITE EVENT

The real hope of such integration rests on a willingness to rethink our theology and to change it where scripture proves that to be necessary. The fundamental requirement of such a revised theology is that it includes all the eight major features of baptism in Spirit we have found in the New Testament, but as aspects of the whole, a *single event*. Any separation of these elements can only, sooner or later, distort and even destroy the 'baptism'.

Some have already had the courage to tackle this task, and I am happy to refer to them while pointing out that we have not yet reached a theology that is completely satisfying when checked with scripture. Two phrases have been coined, which are not strictly scriptural but help to clarify the discussion and point the way forward – 'Spirit baptism' and 'Initiation complex'. One emphasises the 'completeness' and the other the 'incompleteness' of baptism in Spirit.

Complete I am using this word for teaching that does bring together all eight features, which is comparatively hard to find. In fact, I know of no other book where they are specifically listed in the way done here – which was one of the main reasons why I have dared to write yet another volume on the subject.

But a few have clearly been aware of this wholeness and this has led them to stress the fundamental importance of 'Spirit baptism', as they have often called it. They have appreciated its prominent presence in the New Testament and have been burdened by its comparative absence in contemporary churches.

One scholarly but readable example is Professor James D.G. Dunn's *Baptism in the Holy Spirit* (S.C.M., 1970), a pioneering work that deserves far more serious attention than it has received. Here is a full-orbed presentation, based on the equation of 'baptised in' and 'receiving' the Spirit as one and the same thing. As such, he gives it the supreme place in entering the new covenant and the kingdom of God. It is the sine qua non of both, without which the believer is not yet into either. His studies are a fatal blow to 'subsequence', Spirit baptism as a 'second blessing'.

Furthermore, he insists that 'Spirit baptism' was, is and always will be 'a definite, even dramatic, experience'. To say it can be otherwise is a contradiction in terms, like saying water baptism can still be valid without any water.

His 'complete' portrayal of Spirit baptism, combining all its distinctive facets, has not to my knowledge convinced many to change their theology (mine may have even less effect!). That, I believe, is because he overstates his case at a number of points.

The most obvious is the statement that anyone who has not received/been baptised in Spirit is 'not yet a Christian'. That goes further than scripture and therefore too far. I know what he means and agree with that, but it was unfortunate to introduce the word 'Christian' at this juncture, which scripture never does. In fact, both its ancient and modern meanings simply confuse the issue (as we shall see in Chapter 7).

So he states his belief that the Samaritans (in Acts 8) were not 'Christians' until Peter and John prayed for them, though they had believed the gospel and been baptised in the name of Jesus. Now it's one thing to say this in an academic context, but would he preach it from a pulpit? It would decimate his own denomination – and most others!

By the same token, he exalts Spirit baptism at the expense of water baptism, which ceases to be a sacrament, a means of grace, and becomes a mere 'symbol', which says something but does nothing.

All this is a bit 'over the top' and prevented his basic

thesis from having its full impact. As is so often the case, he is right in what he affirms but wrong in what he denies.

Nevertheless, I heartily commend his book to those who think for themselves while they read the thoughts of others. I was thrilled to find such a complete treatment and learned a great deal from it. I have quoted and critiqued it precisely because the courage to challenge firmly-held beliefs is quite rare.

Incomplete I am using this word for the teaching that Spirit baptism is only one element alongside others which are equally important. The phrase which has been coined to describe this perspective is 'initiation complex'. (I'm not sure who originated it, but Michael Harper and David Watson were among the first to use it.) It is a useful term to cover the different features in the beginning of the Christian life which can be considered separately – and indeed must never be identified or confused with each other – but which belong together, with Spirit baptism seen as the final stage and normally close to the others.

The list of separate elements varies a little, but usually boils down to four basics:

> Repenting towards God for sins
> Believing in Jesus as Saviour and Lord
> Being baptised in water
> Receiving/being baptised in Holy Spirit.

I have expanded on these in *The Normal Christian Birth* (Hodder and Stoughton, 1989, republished 1997).

Initiation is here understood as a process which is not complete until all four elements are present, until all four 'events' have happened, until all four actions have been taken.

Though they belong together theologically, they may not come together chronologically. Even in the New Testament there were delays, although as we have pointed out immediate steps were usually taken to remedy the deficiency. Time was not wasted on discussing whether anyone was a 'Christian' or not. That would have been considered an irrelevant debate, wasting time instead of meeting a need. For in those days everyone knew that all the elements were needed. It was the 'apostles' doctrine' in which they 'steadfastly continued'. No one asked: 'Can they be called Christians yet?' They would only have asked: 'Have they repented yet? Have they believed yet? Have they been baptised yet? Have they received the Spirit yet?'

It is crucial to such an understanding to state clearly that water baptism and Spirit baptism are *not* the same thing, that believing in Jesus and receiving the Spirit are *not* the same thing. None of the separate elements in the 'complex' of initiation can be taken for granted. None happen automatically because the others have; and none can happen unconsciously.

I believe that only such an approach gives the same significance and importance to each element that it receives in the New Testament. In particular, Spirit baptism, instead of being the neglected factor, takes its proper place as the climax and confirmation of the other three.

I also believe that anyone coming with an open mind to scripture, free of prejudice and tradition, will come to much the same understanding. Baptism in Spirit must be kept complete, with all its biblical features held firmly together, yet it must be seen as incomplete without repentance, faith and baptism (in water).

I don't believe that all the reasons for the rejection of this understanding are theological. Certainly there is a reluctance to change beliefs in all three 'camps', sacramental, evangelical and pentecostal, none of which have even accepted all eight features of Spirit baptism. And until there is a willingness to rethink these positions in the light of scripture, they will remain separate streams with little unity between them. For the differences concern the most fundamental question: 'How does one become a Christian?' and even more basic: 'What is a Christian?'

But I have found that at the grass roots level (the local church) even those who are convinced that the 'initiation complex' outlined above is true to the New Testament are nevertheless extremely reluctant to apply it, and therefore hold back from preaching it. The practical problems they would have to work through are too daunting. One final chapter will face these squarely and, I hope, offer some help and encouragement to pastors and evangelists facing this dilemma.

7

The Practical Problems

So far in this volume we have been giving primary attention to the theology of Spirit baptism, because that is where all lasting change must begin. Unless and until the Church has a united conviction, solidly based on scripture, the different streams will continue on their separate ways indefinitely.

But theology must, sooner or later, be practised and experienced if it is to be of any real value. An academic debate is of little significance unless it is translated into action. That is when the major problems arise!

The conclusions we have presented here, from studying the relevant New Testament data, are midway between evangelical and pentecostal positions. Both have been commended for some features and criticised for others. A combination of the best insights of each has been offered, not as a compromise but as a more comprehensive presentation which could, and should, provide a point of biblical integration for both – and one which could also bring in the sacramental stream, if they too are willing to re-examine their assumptions.

'No man's land', between opposing forces, can be a lonely place. It can also be a dangerous place, open to attack from both sides! But it is also the place where an armistice can be signed and agreements worked out to unite in a lasting peace. That is the hope, admittedly slender, behind the writing of this book, with the full awareness that none of the existing streams will find it wholly to their liking.

However, in this chapter, we approach the task from a very different angle. It is written for those, a growing number, who are convinced that the 'initiation complex' view is biblically sound – and indeed is the only one doing full justice to the New Testament – but who see almost insuperable obstacles in the way of applying it in practice to the Church today. Of course, to believe in one way and to have to behave in another is a rich source of stress and guilt, to say nothing of hypocrisy. Nevertheless, I meet an increasing number of pastors and clergy caught between their conscience and their congregation on this and other matters.

As one vicar said to me: 'I agree with what you are teaching, but daren't teach it myself; I've got enough problems in my church without adding any more!' Another vicar did teach it, with some unexpected results ('We've never had such harmony'), but told me he hadn't dared to inform the bishop of what he'd been saying and doing! Practical politics can have an influence, as well as sound doctrine.

The fact is that the contemporary Church has moved a long way away from the 'apostles' doctrine', and for a long time, which presents a double barrier to its restoration. A motorist who asked a pedestrian for directions to his destination received the disconcerting reply: 'If I wanted to go there, I wouldn't start from here.' That is exactly our practical dilemma.

Nothing less than reformation is needed and that has always been resisted by those with a vested interest in the status quo. Traditions die hard, especially in the sphere of religion, often the one unchanging feature in a constantly changing scene and therefore a symbol and source of security. Brave souls attempting reform soon discover its painful price. They will only be honoured after their work has been widely accepted – if they look for human rather than divine approval.

The situation calls for courageous pioneers who have come to new (and yet old) convictions and are willing to preach and practise them, whatever the cost or consequence, refusing to be deflected by practical problems.

There are two areas of difficulty facing any who seek to apply what has been said in this book (but they must not 'try it out' as an experiment – only after being absolutely convinced, by scripture and the Spirit, of the truth).

One 'problem' is pastoral and arises when facing believers with this truth. The other is evangelistic, affecting our methods of outreach to unbelievers.

BELIEVERS

Complacent As soon as the need for baptism in Spirit is mentioned in the presence of those who already regard themselves as Christians, an immediate and emotive reaction is the usual result, especially if it is described as we have done, taking the pattern in the book of Acts as a norm rather than later traditions of the Church.

Many church members, perhaps most, will find this extremely threatening and respond with some indignation. 'Are you saying I'm not a Christian? That I shouldn't be a member of this church? That I'm not saved? That I won't go to heaven when I die?'

It is not easy, in the heat of such a reaction, to hold a rational discussion. But patient teaching is needed to unravel the premises underlying such questions, which prevent the answers from being given, much less received.

For example, the word 'Christian' actually confuses all debates on this issue. It is used only three times in scripture and then as a nickname given by outsiders. It is not a helpful term for insiders, especially with its popular modern connotation – someone who is safe from hell and has a ticket to heaven. It is commonly used as a synonym for 'saved'.

'Saved' is also misleading, since it is almost universally used in the past tense as a synonym for 'converted' or 'born again', as something already accomplished in a moment, over and done with, settled for ever, whereas in the New Testament salvation is a process taking time, expressed in three tenses (have been, are being and will be saved).

To put all this in a visual context, both 'Christian' and 'saved' are used as if they correspond to one side of a *vertical* line to be crossed, from being an 'unsaved non-Christian'. When this is the concept of salvation, repentance and faith (which the 'unsaved' need) are on the left side of the line, whereas water and Spirit baptism are on the right side (needed by those already 'saved' and therefore not a necessary part of their salvation!). This is to put asunder what God has joined together.

Salvation in the New Testament is more a *horizontal* line, a 'road to be travelled' (the earliest label was not 'Christianity', but 'the Way'; Acts 16:17; 18:26; 19:9, 23; 24:14). Repentance, faith, water baptism and Spirit baptism are the first four steps on the Way – all four are necessary to full salvation and there are many other steps to follow. Perhaps this is why the most common term for a follower of Jesus in the book of Acts is 'disciple', which can be used of those who have taken just one step (Acts 19:1) and of all who are travelling on the Way, however far they may have gone (Acts 9:26).

But what if someone dies before reaching the end of the journey? It is strange that so many of these questions betray a morbid interest in how death will affect their salvation rather than a healthy interest in how salvation will affect their life! That is due to a greater interest in being safe from hell than being saved from sins (though the latter was the primary reason why Jesus came and died for us; Matt. 1:21; 2 Cor. 5:15, 21), as if the gospel is first and foremost an insurance policy covering risks in the next world.

We have already said that the apostles never wasted time on discussing what was the state or status of those who had repented, believed and been baptised but had not received the Spirit. They simply remedied the deficiency as quickly as possible. The reason we have so much debate is that there are so many today who are in the same situation as the Samaritans (or even more deficient, lacking water baptism) and who have been like that for so long, sometimes years.

So let us grasp the nettle and give a straight answer. It is much easier to do so when the vertical concept of salvation has been discarded in favour of the horizontal Way. I believe that anyone who is already on the Way of salvation and travelling in the right direction is safe with the Lord if they die. If any Samaritan had died before Peter and John got there, I'm sure they would be in heaven. If someone had only repented and believed but not yet been able to be baptised in water or Spirit, I still have no doubt. I even believe there are scriptural grounds for thinking that if anyone genuinely repents of their sins and is seeking the mercy of God, they will be accepted (Acts 10:34-5). All those who have begun to walk the Way and died before they could get any further will, I believe, be with the Lord in Paradise (the dying thief is my proof; Luke 23:43). Whenever I make this point, I think of a ninety-two-year-old lady we took into our church retirement home. She didn't even realise her family had put her in a Christian home, but her faculties and activities were still there. She had been Britain's champion lady rifle shot and went jogging daily! She soon put her faith in Christ and we fixed the date for her baptism (by immersion), but she went to heaven just days before.

But the dying must not be used as a standard, much less an excuse, for the living. The dying thief would probably be horrified that his case had been used as a doctrine of the minimal admission fee to heaven for those with plenty of life in front of them. We should pity, not envy, him because he couldn't have it all and will never have the reward of faithful service. He is an encouragement for the dying, but not for the living.

Even those who have had both water and Spirit baptism are not 'safe' yet – and won't be unless they keep walking along the Way until they, too, cross the Jordan of death. This is the whole message of Bunyan's *The Pilgrim's Progress*. Some may be surprised to know that both Calvinists and Arminians are agreed that the living need to persevere in faith and press on to holiness if final salvation is to be reached; they only differ on why some fail to reach that destination (see my *Once Saved, Always Saved?*, Hodder and Stoughton, 1996).

We can go a little further. Forgiveness of sins is not connected with Spirit baptism in the New Testament. It is linked with repentance, faith and water baptism. Therefore a person could go to heaven as a forgiven sinner, justified by faith, before receiving the Holy Spirit. But without the latter, there would be no proof that they had done so, since the gift of the Spirit is the 'seal', the mark of God's ownership.

Nor must we assume that the Holy Spirit is a complete stranger before he is 'received'. It is his task to convict people of sin, righteousness and judgment, leading to repentance and faith. But all this can happen without a full awareness of his person, even while benefiting from his work. There is some analogy here with the experience of the twelve apostles: 'he has been *with* you and will be *in* you' (John 14:17).

What we must not assume is that this work means either that he has already been 'received' or that he already 'indwells'. Both these terms are kept for Spirit baptism in the New Testament, and should be today. Paul's question is still valid: 'Having believed, did you receive Holy Spirit?' (Acts 19:2). But the implications of the question must be spelled out very clearly to avoid hasty conclusions and wrong reactions. It can involve a radical re-education of what 'salvation' really means, in terms of admission to holiness before heaven.

However, when all is said and done, complacent 'disciples' (put that way, it seems a contradiction in terms, so we'd better say 'complacent Christians') always object to being told they need more than they've got already. The 'ticket to heaven' mentality has such a deep hold that it requires continual chipping away before it is dislodged. It comes as a shock to be told that without holiness no one will see the Lord (Heb. 12:14). And who can reach that holiness which is acceptable to the Lord without first being drenched in holy Spirit? To try and achieve it any other way is to finish up as a Pharisee, full of the filthy 'dung' of self-righteousness (Phil. 3:7-11).

The necessary re-education must include the transfer of focus from death to life. Evangelists may have been partly responsible for the present emphasis on when we die rather than how we live. A biblical balance needs to be recovered – to be safe from hell is for those who are eager and willing to be saved from their sins here and now, from their power as well as the penalty. Admission to heaven requires holiness as well as forgiveness from the living, whatever concession is made for the dying.

To sum up, the complacent need to be challenged with the necessity of baptism in Spirit if they are going to live a saved life, take their full role in the body of Christ and be fully available to serve the needs of others.

Frustrated There is another group of believers among whom difficulties may arise. These have accepted the need to be baptised in Spirit, have sought this but have failed to 'receive'. They know their need but are frustrated that it has not been met.

It does seem more difficult to catch up on what they should have had at the beginning. Having managed to be a 'Christian' for so long without this experience, it is less easy to make room for it by 'simple' faith. There are two aspects to the problem.

Positively, there is need for an active co-operation in 'receiving'. No one will ever have an overflow from the mouth unless they speak out. The Spirit gives utterance, but doesn't do the speaking. Sometimes, if the mouth is not used, the welling up within causes an emotional outburst (sobbing or even laughter), but the Spirit of prophecy wants the tongue (that little thing formerly set on fire by hell; Jas. 3:6). Most of the later gifts the 'baptised' will use are gifts of speech (words of wisdom, words of knowledge, words of prophecy, words in another language, words of interpretation). If there is an initial reluctance to allow the Spirit to control the tongue, the other gifts are less likely to follow. Those who have always kept a tight control of their speech, as well as those who have become accustomed to a passive role in spiritual matters, are likely to have problems in obeying the Lord's imperative: 'Receive!' (John 20:22).

Negatively, there are fears and inhibitions that hold the blessing back. I have mentioned these and offered advice about dealing with them elsewhere (in *The Normal Christian Birth*, chapter 35), so will not repeat all that here. They will need to be dealt with firmly and sensitively before offering ministry.

Should there still be a failure to 'receive', there may be a need to go 'back to basics', two in particular.

On the one hand, we need to check out that there has been real repentance (in word and deed as well as thought), 'working faith' (and not just profession) and baptism in water (according to scripture).

On the other hand, we need to make sure that there is an independent conviction, based on scripture rather than observation or testimony, that baptism in Spirit is something that Jesus can give and every believer can have. People need to be sure what to expect and of their own expectancy. And they need to be reminded that faith is not content with asking once or twice, but will *go on* asking, seeking and knocking until the prayer is answered (Luke 11:9-13). Clearly this involves new dimensions of pastoral care of those already in the Church. But we also need to consider the necessary changes in our dealings with those we seek to bring into the Church.

UNBELIEVERS

Twentieth-century evangelism was heavily influenced by nineteenth-century American revivalism, which tended to over-simplify the appropriate reception of the gospel. Invariably, an appeal was made at the end of a public meeting for those who wanted to make a response to come to the platform area (the 'altar call') and there 'make a commitment' by repeating phrase by phrase a petition voiced by the preacher (the 'sinner's prayer'). The 'enquirers' would then be 'counselled', on the assumption that they had now 'received' Christ into their heart and life and needed only a few texts from scripture to assure them they were now 'born again', together with advice about keeping it up by reading the Bible, praying and joining a church. The public aspect was not strictly necessary (the 'sinners' prayer' was included in many publications so that it could be used privately) but was considered desirable.

The gaps in this general technique are very significant. Since it was all covered quite quickly at the end of a meeting, often late in the evening, there was simply not enough time for any deeds to prove repentance (Luke 3:8; Acts 26:20), or for more than a profession of faith. Above all, neither baptism in water nor baptism in Spirit played any part in 'becoming a Christian'. By New Testament teaching and practice, this is seriously inadequate, falling far short of the 'initiation complex' we found there.

While it cannot be denied that many have got started this way, they have often taken a long time making up the deficit, some never doing so. And we must face the fact that very many starting like this fall away soon afterwards – and are very, very hard to recover for a 'second go at it' (the frequent response is: 'I tried it and it didn't work').

It is my observation and experience that those who get all four biblical elements of initiation close together at the very beginning of their Christian life are far less likely to fall away and far more likely to grow and develop with the least help from others. We could save ourselves a good deal of anxiety and after-care by being better midwives when assisting at the new birth. And just as babies have to be washed clean and often have to be helped to breathe (usually with the laying on of hands!), so those who are born again need the spiritual equivalents.

Few changes would make our evangelism more effective than the restoration of the two baptisms, in water and in Spirit, to the place they once had in the apostolic mission.

Baptised in water   We have already noted that the transfer of baptism to infants was probably the main cause of the declining experience of Spirit baptism, which had survived while adult catechumens were prepared for immersion.

We have also mentioned that the most appropriate and the most effective time to pray for someone to 'receive the Spirit' is immediately after their immersion in water.

In the New Testament there is a clear and close association between water and Spirit baptisms, though they are never identified or confused with each other, never happening at the same moment. Something seems to be lost when they are widely separated.

Jesus didn't tell us to get people to make a 'decision' for him or a 'commitment' to him, nor did he command us to persuade others to 'give their heart' to him or 'invite him into their lives'. These and many other quaint euphemisms have taken the place of his Great Commission to 'go and make *disciples* of all nations [ethnic groups, not states], *baptising* them . . .' (Matt. 28:19). That is how we get them started.

Why, then, do we not baptise those who repent and believe in response to our gospel preaching? On most 'foreign' mission fields, this is normal (most Anglican cathedrals overseas have baptistries, pools for adult immersion). But in Western civilisations, which some still dare to call 'Christendom', so many have been christened as babies (still over half in the United Kingdom) that churches relying on this as their major recruitment (technically known as 'biological growth' but more bluntly described as 'getting hold of them before they can object'!) would protest vigorously or simply refuse to join in any united outreach.

So what are the chances of baptism being restored to its normal and central place in evangelism (as in Acts 2:41; 8:12; 10:48; 19:5)? Actually, quite good, but more by default than decision. The fastest growing streams of the Church throughout the world usually limit baptism to penitent believers. Even in those countries where this has not been the case, especially in Europe and those parts of the world receiving missionaries from Europe, the christening of babies is in serious decline. Secularised culture in Western society is more and more akin to a pagan mission field. In fact, it increasingly resembles the declining Roman Empire, in spite of all the technological advances. In such a situation 'biological growth' has to be replaced by 'conversion growth', as in the days of the early Church.

So we can expect to see an increase in 'adult' baptisms, making it easier to associate it with the reception of the Spirit – baptism and confirmation rolled into one event (the 'confirmation' will be divine rather than human, even though hands are laid on).

Baptised in Spirit This would also make possible a return to the practice of the early Church, including the pre-baptism instruction teaching about the Spirit, creating an expectancy that God himself will take part in their 'initiation'.

But before such instruction could be given, there would have to be some real changes in all three major streams of the Church.

The *sacramental* stream would have to distinguish the two baptisms clearly from each other, accepting that in the Bible water baptism is neither simultaneous nor synonymous with Spirit baptism. Both need to become part of the candidate's experience.

The *evangelical* stream would have to distinguish clearly between believing in Jesus and receiving the Spirit, breaking the habit of using the unbiblical term 'receive Jesus', never used in post-Pentecost evangelism.

The *pentecostal* stream would have to relinquish the unbiblical notion of two 'receptions' of the Spirit, one 'subsequent' to initiation, though this is probably the least radical change of the three.

All three would need to give clear and positive teaching about how the Spirit is given and received, why he needs to be received and, above all, that Jesus is the baptiser in Spirit no matter who baptises the candidates in water. They can start asking for this 'good gift' from the Father by the Son even before their baptism in water, in faith that it will be theirs immediately after.

They should be told how the Spirit of prophecy will manifest his presence, so they know what to expect and can co-operate with him as soon as they experience his coming upon them. They should not be told to believe 'it' has happened when nothing has happened. This is no kind of a 'seal'.

Such are some of the guidelines for an outline of

evangelism that would be much nearer the practice of the apostles and could be expected to lead to similar results: churches of new disciples able remarkably soon to reproduce themselves (Acts 9:31; 16:5).

What we are advocating has come to be known in some circles as 'the Peter package'. That is, to discard John 1:12 and Revelation 3:20 as our stock-in-trade texts for counselling enquirers and to use instead the more appropriate words of Peter on the day of Pentecost: 'Repent and be baptised, every one of you, in the name of Jesus Christ for the forgiveness of your sins; and you will receive the gift of the Holy Spirit' (Acts 2:38).

The practical problems facing us today, both inside and outside the Church, are considerable but not insuperable. If we set our wills to overcome them, God will supply the power.

Epilogue

The thoughtful reader will surely have been left with one simple question: if, for most of its history, the Church has not been preaching a full biblical doctrine of Spirit baptism, how do we explain the work of the Spirit down through the ages, in individuals and fellowships? Indeed, the Spirit has clearly been at work where there has been no mention at all of 'receiving' the Spirit.

I believe the answer is that *God is above his Word*. He is free to act in any way he chooses, consistent with his character. He is a God of grace, which means that he is a generous God.

Unique among the world religions, Christianity puts justification before sanctification. We don't need to be righteous before we are accepted as his sons – which is just as well, since that is beyond our capability. He accepts us on the ground of faith in order that we might become righteous by continuing in that faith.

So we don't need to be *morally* perfect before we can receive his blessings. Neither do we need to be *mentally* perfect either. Thank God he does not wait until our doctrine is right before his Spirit works on us.

Anyone seeking his power and purity, his love and

peace, however they express this longing, whether they can quote texts to support it or not, is likely to have their prayer answered. I have met many who have clearly been baptised in Spirit but who were ignorant of the relevant scriptures and did not realise what was happening to them.

God *wants* to give the gifts and fruit of the Spirit and responds to the sincere hunger and thirst of any believer, whether or not they can articulate their desire in doctrinal and biblical words. That is why Paul spoke about 'renewal by the Holy Spirit, whom he poured out on us *generously* through Jesus Christ our Saviour' (Titus 3:5-6).

If we waited until we got everything right, either morally or mentally, we'd receive nothing from his hand. He blesses us in spite of what we are rather than because of what we are – provided we believe in him.

That is why his Spirit has worked in the very different streams – Puritan and pentecostal, Catholic and Protestant, evangelical and charismatic. The Spirit is active before there is theological agreement. The dynamic precedes the doctrine. Those who have *the Spirit* are to 'make every effort to keep the unity of the Spirit through the bond of peace – until we all reach unity in *the faith* and in the knowledge of the Son of God and become mature' (Eph. 4:3, 13).

So God, being above his Word, can act beyond his Word, though never in contradiction to it. However, two very mistaken conclusions are often drawn from his gracious generosity.

First, it is too easily assumed that his blessing is the approval of our teaching, that because his Holy Spirit is working our doctrinal understanding must be correct. This by no means follows. His blessing means that he is gracious, not that we are accurate. We have already said enough to establish this.

Second, and far more serious, is the assumption that doctrine is not important, that sincerity is all that matters. Why argue about theology if God is going to bless anyway? The post-modern culture favours tolerant relativism and hates intolerant dogmatism. Could we not learn from this and rejoice in the experience of the Spirit, whatever is taught about it?

Of course, from this epilogue so far it could even be concluded that writing this book has been a sheer waste of time. Why plead for a united theology if it really doesn't matter? Why not stay with the pragmatic principle: if the teaching 'works', whatever is taught, why not leave it alone and simply agree to differ? Surely the cause of ecumenical unity would be better served by such unbigoted goodwill, free from all mutual criticism?

First of all, God may be above his Word but *we are under his Word*. He has given us this revelation as the final standard for all matters of belief and behaviour. It is to be constantly used as a touchstone to measure all deviations.

Those who teach in the body of Christ have an awesome responsibility to give an accurate exposition and appropriate application of the scriptures, because those 'who teach will be judged more strictly' (Jas. 3:1). That is because of the extra burden of guilt at having misled others as well as being mistaken themselves. That is why Paul exhorts Timothy to 'Do your best to present yourself to God as one approved who does not need to be ashamed and who correctly handles the word of truth' (2 Tim. 2:15; quoted earlier, but well worth repeating).

We all have this duty to be true to scripture in what we say and do. Even as I write this, I am praying: 'Please God, if anything I have written is not true to your Word, may your Spirit of truth warn the reader not to accept it, lest it damage their walk with you, Amen.'

So there is a *negative* reason for re-examining our traditional or habitual interpretation of passages relating to Spirit baptism (which is why Chapter 3, on the New Testament, is by far the longest). We need to avoid giving others either a false security or a false expectancy on this issue. But we must not fear doing this to the point of it becoming a phobia, paralysing us into saying nothing at all.

Which brings me to the *positive* reason for this study. Only when preachers offer God's gifts with clarity and confidence do their hearers reach out in faith for them. Opinions don't get this response. Convictions do. We only promise to others what we are deeply convinced God has promised in his Word.

But we have seen that baptism in Spirit is one of the benefits of our salvation in Christ that is directly associated with the word 'promise' (Luke 24:49; Acts 1:4; 2:33,39). It is a promise that may be confidently proclaimed, having already been so widely fulfilled. It is sad that it has been so muted in Christian preaching and teaching.

The world has yet to see how much more power, purity and unity there would be throughout the Church if all her streams were declaring as loudly and clearly as John the baptiser: 'We baptise you in water, but Jesus will baptise you in holy Spirit.'

My hope and prayer is for just such a united witness to Jesus the baptiser before he returns to reign. May this book play a small part in helping to bring that about, for the good of the Church and the glory of the Lord.

Printed in Great Britain
by Amazon